To Jane —
I hope you learn
how to cook ! :)

T·E·X·A·S

Q

xoxo,
Cheryl Alters Jamison

CHERYL ALTERS JAMISON

AUTHOR OF THE BEST-SELLING *SMOKE & SPICE*

T·E·X·A·S

100 RECIPES

FOR THE VERY BEST BARBECUE
❖ FROM THE LONE STAR STATE ❖
ALL SMOKE-COOKED TO PERFECTION

HARVARD COMMON PRESS

Inspiring | Educating | Creating | Entertaining

Brimming with creative inspiration, how-to projects, and useful information to enrich your everyday life, Quarto Knows is a favorite destination for those pursuing their interests and passions. Visit our site and dig deeper with our books into your area of interest: Quarto Creates, Quarto Cooks, Quarto Homes, Quarto Lives, Quarto Drives, Quarto Explores, Quarto Gifts, or Quarto Kids.

First Published in 2020 by The Harvard Common Press, an imprint of The Quarto Group, 100 Cummings Center, Suite 265-D, Beverly, MA 01915, USA.
T (978) 282-9590 F (978) 283-2742 QuartoKnows.com

The Harvard Common Press titles are also available at discount for retail, wholesale, promotional, and bulk purchase. For details, contact the Special Sales Manager by email at specialsales@quarto.com or by mail at The Quarto Group, Attn: Special Sales Manager, 100 Cummings Center, Suite 265-D, Beverly, MA 01915, USA.

24 23 22 21 20   1 2 3 4 5

ISBN: 978-1-55832-971-3

Digital edition published in 2020
eISBN: 978-1-55832-972-0

Library of Congress Cataloging-in-Publication Data

Names: Jamison, Cheryl Alters, author.
Title: Texas Q : 100 recipes for the very best barbecue from the Lone Star
   State, all smoke-cooked to perfection / Cheryl Alters Jamison.
Description: Beverly : Harvard Common Press, [2020] | Includes index. |
   Summary: "The only book on Texas barbecue that goes beyond beef and
   brisket to cover pork, lamb, chicken, and seafood, celebrating the true
   variety of genuine Texas Q"-- Provided by publisher.
Identifiers: LCCN 2019050081 (print) | LCCN 2019050082 (ebook) | ISBN
   9781558329713 (trade paperback) | ISBN 9781558329720 (ebook)
Subjects: LCSH: Barbecuing--Texas. | LCGFT: Cookbooks.
Classification: LCC TX840.B3 J363 2020 (print) | LCC TX840.B3 (ebook) |
   DDC 641.7/609764--dc23
LC record available at https://lccn.loc.gov/2019050081
LC ebook record available at https://lccn.loc.gov/2019050082

Design: Rick Landers Miller
Page Layout: Megan Jones
Photography: Gabriella Marks, except pages 2, 14, 24, and 64 Shutterstock
Chef du Livre: Mike Whistler
Illustration: Shutterstock

Printed in China

For Bill—

The fire still burns.

CONTENTS

PREFACE: My Texas Barbecue Journey

I was not born to Texas barbecue. As a kid growing up in central Illinois, I was familiar with the term used for grilled food and for meat that was tomato saucy and surrounded by a bun, something like a sloppy Joe. I had an early epiphany with true Q on a family trip through Georgia. I got a sandwich that initially horrified me—pork instead of beef, with a thin vinegar sauce that maybe had mustard in it too. Astoundingly, coleslaw was plopped *on* the sandwich, not beside it. I have to admit that I didn't eat much of it—just enough so my parents wouldn't complain that I was wasting food. I just couldn't wrap my head around it. But, I never forgot that sandwich.

A few years later, in the late 1970s, I found myself living in Dallas. A boyfriend of the era was an aficionado of Central Texas barbecue. He loved to regale me with stories about how down in Lockhart, true Q joints served just meat on butcher paper with maybe white bread or onions or dill pickles on the side. If this didn't sound strange enough, he then broke it to me that there was no sauce—none. In that heyday of TGI Fridays and fern bars, I couldn't imagine anything that sounded less likely a destination for a food-related field trip.

Nonetheless, the day came for that first visit to Lockhart, to the holy grail of the original Kreutz's, with its raw umber patina of smoke. When I walked in, it smelled promising. A depression in the floor held a wafting wood fire that seemed impossibly far away from where the meat was supposedly cooking. The boyfriend ordered some beef by the pound. Slices came with what I saw as a scorched, crusty surface. I wondered how this meat was so "burned" when such a wisp of a fire was the source of the heat. By this time, though, the aroma was totally intoxicating. I was coaxed into tasting a bite topped with the craggy surface, or bark, I thought was the burned stuff. The explosion of meaty succulence, of texture, of smoke, was an epiphany. It was as immediately satisfying as that long-ago Georgia sandwich had been disturbing.

So began my immersion and education in Texas barbecue. I think Cooper's in Llano came next, where the meat was plucked from big metal boxes outdoors. Each was the size of a chest freezer and had the same kind of prop-up lid. After pointing out the meat we wanted and how much of it, the pit boss on hand would dunk it in a vat of liquid, not quite a sauce by my interpretation. Even though I was somewhat distrustful of sausage, we made a pilgrimage to Luling. City Market cranked out links of something called unpromisingly, to my mind at least, "hot guts." Again, I was won over by the coarse meat's spicy heat fusing with smoke and the juices dripping down my chin.

Next came Louie Mueller's in Taylor. As I exited the screen door, after sampling what I considered to be the most amazing collection of meats I had had anywhere, I thought I was starting to get a sense of this Texas tradition. Yet, I still had a ways to go to grasp the complexity of this elemental form of cooking.

Back in Dallas, I began making the trek to Sonny Bryan's stand on Inwood for an early lunch before they ran out of meat. Like everybody else, I either sat at one of the school desks inside or stood against my car door in my heels and business dress to eat chopped beef sandwiches. Here, you could get some tangy rusty-looking sauce, but it didn't taste like the tomatoey liquid called barbecue sauce in grocery stores of the day.

The boyfriend took a job in Louisiana, so I found myself driving many weekends through East Texas, where the barbecue turned out to be very different at places like Bodacious Bar-B-Q in Longview and Country Tavern in Kilgore. I was to learn that the influences came from the Deep South and often from the African-American tradition that was focused more on pork ribs and ladles full of sauce. I found too that what I thought of as Louisiana Cajun flavors didn't stop at the state line.

My many-splendored tour of Texas barbecue took a hiatus when I was offered a career-related move to Santa Fe, New Mexico, in 1980. To feed my barbecue passion, I succumbed to advertising and purchased a small domed vertical cooker, called a water smoker then and often referred to now as a bullet smoker. Trying to get a combination of charcoal and wood chips ignited in it long enough to cook something as small and quick as a chicken breast, much less anything more substantial, was nigh impossible. It seemed as worthless and clunky as a pair of cowboy boots on a ballerina. After a season of futzing around with it, I hauled it to my village dump in total exasperation. Some years later, I decided that little smoker hadn't been a total piece of crap, but the instructions for using it had been.

By that time, I had settled down with another barbecue-loving Texas guy, my late husband, Bill. At the time, we were writing a book that would become *Texas Home Cooking*. We had been driving around Texas on a late-winter trip, finding inspiration and ideas for the book as a whole. The way we were going to deal with preparing barbecue, the national food of the Lone Star State, was weighing on us. In sampling the attempts of friends, family, and even ourselves, we had become pretty convinced that home cooks should really leave barbecue to seasoned professional pitmasters, sages of smoked meat such as Bobby Mueller of Louie Mueller's and Roy Perez of Kreutz's. We were even toying with printing a "recipe" for Texas barbecue that said "hit the highway and make your way to Mueller's or Kreutz's," or to other well-regarded joints of the day. At the time, there were no books that explained the process well. Publishers weren't roaming the barbecue landscape looking to give pitmasters book contracts. There was no Internet or YouTube with how-to videos. Aaron Franklin, today's reigning barbecue star, was in high school. However, a guy named Wayne Whitworth was about to shake up our whole mindset.

We'd noticed a small recurring ad in *Texas Monthly* for barbecue pits made in Houston by Pitts & Spitts. Arriving in Houston, I called the company and explained that we were collecting information on proper smoking techniques for a Texas cookbook. I was transferred right to honcho Wayne. I was impressed to be connected right to the top but found out during the conversation that, save the receptionist, Wayne was literally the only one there at the factory/warehouse/office headquarters. Everyone else was over at the gargantuan World's Championship Bar-B-Que Contest, held annually in conjunction with the Houston Livestock Show and Rodeo. I'm pretty sure Wayne was a little lonesome sitting

there on his own. He said to come right over. We did. We convinced him that we were serious about explaining this barbecue cooking to the greater culinary world if we could figure out how to do it ourselves. He convinced us that, with one of his pits, we could turn tough-as-a-saddle beef brisket into the food of the gods. Furthermore, he announced that he would drive that pit some 880 miles (1416 km) to us and make sure we learned the right way to do Q.

This is how, on an auspicious May Day in 1993, we were set up with a load of oak logs, plenty of food that could soak up smoke, and beer—lots of beer. The hardwood logs needed to fuel the incoming Pitts & Spitts barbecue pit had been a lot harder to come by than the beer. Most people in Santa Fe, New Mexico, at 7,000 feet (2 km) in the southern Rocky Mountains, burn piñon, a soft but strongly aromatic pine that grows in the area. It burns hot and fast with a lot of pitch, exactly the opposite of what is required for barbecue. I called restaurants around town that claimed to offer smoked or wood-grilled dishes on their menus. We got leads on mesquite, but it burned hotter than we wanted for our first attempts at serious Central Texas–style barbecue. The "chef" at a then-well-known rib chain told me that there was no need to find real wood. All I had to do was drown the meat in liquid smoke and bake it. Finally, I found a purveyor of piñon who also scavenged oak. We were ready for what was about to become our first weeklong barbecue.

Wayne rolled into town with our new offset-firebox smoker secured firmly in his pickup bed. Bill and Wayne drove down by the state Department of Labor, where guys hung out looking for work, and found some well-muscled dudes willing to get this 800-pound (363-kg) beauty of heavy-duty cast-iron and stainless steel off the truck. Wayne was a barbecue wizard. He knew every nuance of the pit he brought us and taught us how to cook everything from brisket to ribs to what is still talked about today as the $100 fish.

It didn't take long after that for Bill and me to ring our patio with some fourteen different cookers for smoking and barbecue. They stayed in place for so long that friends considered them an art installation.

From those experiences, we wrote the barbecue chapter of *Texas Home Cooking* but knew we needed to tell a much broader story. That bigger story became *Smoke & Spice*, a book that won us our first James Beard Foundation book award, has stayed in print for some twenty-five years, and sold more than 1.5 million copies. Just those facts alone bear witness to barbecue—the food, its traditions, its culture—getting a new lease on life. It's been so darned exciting to see the expansion of the professional barbecue community, but it's also a good time to put together a new collection of recipes for home cooks and backyard barbecuers that reflects what's occurring statewide. I'm a little grayer around my hairline, but I'm still smoking. Let's dig into the heart of Texas Q together.

BRAGGING RIGHTS TEXAS BBQ

CHAPTER 1

Q'D UP:
THE RESURRECTION OF
A ONCE-DYING ART

Briskets, butts, burnt ends, beef ribs, pork ribs, and sandwiches stacked high with housemade sausage and housemade pickles on a housemade bun. Barbecue sauce enlivened with just-pulled espresso. Tex-Mex and barbecue melded in bountiful pulled pollo tacos. German burritos, Vietnamese pho, and spring rolls loaded with barbecued meats. Thai green curry flavoring Cajun boudin. Texas Q is a many-splendored thing.

It wasn't always so.

A BITE OF HISTORY

Way back in the 1990s when my late husband, Bill Jamison, and I wrestled with how to approach barbecue in *Texas Home Cooking*, it seemed to be a dying art, respected but pretty much the province of aging pitmasters in far-flung rural communities. Frank Stewart, who, with Lolis Eric Elie, was putting together *Smokestack Lightning*, a book capturing the spirit of barbecue at that same time, said it succinctly: "what we have here is a dinosaur without a mate."

Venerable pitmasters were retiring or passing away. Health departments were making increasingly onerous rules for a cooking form that already took hours in an era of microwave ovens and minute rice. However, companies like Pitts & Spitts had begun making sleek commercial versions of the old DIY oil-drum backyard smokers. These smokers actually worked well, if someone could tell the public how they worked and what could be barbecued in them. Pitts & Spitts was just one of the companies that at one time fabricated equipment for the oil industry before times had gotten lean. While things were looking grim for barbecue joints and their proprietors, there was hope for backyard cooks with this new generation of equipment. We got so excited about the possibilities that after penning that small chapter on barbecue for the Texas cookbook, we went all in on barbecue with a whole tome on the topic, *Smoke & Spice*. It was our attempt to entice backyard cooks to Q, while recognizing many of the commercial practitioners who were still plugging away at the craft in their smoke-stained joints.

A funny thing happened, though, on the way to barbecue's demise. In a combination of circumstances—a fascination with live-fire cooking, artisanal foods, sustainable agricultural practices, and our own American culinary heritage mashed up against a recession that kicked off the flourishing of food trucks, "fine dining" chefs branching out into more casual dining forms, and perhaps even the writings of folks like ourselves—Q made a comeback bigger than the Houston Astros with Alex Bregman.

CHANGING FACES AND PLACES

In Texas, in particular, where everything's bigger, bolder, and sometimes brasher, the unlikely leader of the renaissance was a mild-mannered bespectacled young man who had only just begun to experiment with barbecue. Aaron Franklin's intense attention to detail, uncanny ability to imagine, build, and fine-tune equipment for the ultimate cook, and insistence on high-quality, well-raised meat raised the bar in such a way that his name and his Franklin Barbecue in Austin are synonymous with Texas Q. Aaron's James Beard Foundation award as Best Chef Southwest also furthered the recognition of the entire barbecue community.

He and his wife, Stacy, are among a number of younger couples who have jumped into this business in more recent years, joined by Emma and Travis Heim at Heim Barbecue in Fort Worth, partners Diane and Justin Fourton of Pecan Lodge in Dallas, and Misty and Todd David of Cattleack Barbeque in Dallas. Down in Austin, Catherine and Shane Stiles have Stiles Switch Barbeque. Catherine also runs BarbecueWife.com, a super-stylish site full of interviews with other barbecue wives and products Catherine sells, like Bloody Mary mix that incorporates their barbecue sauce. Modesty and Miguel Vidal own Valentina's Tex-Mex Barbecue in Austin and offer tacos and other traditional Tex-Mex dishes made with smoked meats.

Down in Brownsville at Vera's, the Vera family has the only commercial earthen pit in the ground where chopped beef barbacoa is made from entire cow heads barbecued in classic Mexican fashion. Grandfathered in under older, more lenient health department rules, this venerable establishment has had a new boost in recognition. Can you believe that the *ojos*, or eyeballs, of a cow are so popular these days that it's recommended you call ahead and reserve one? In San Antonio, Esaul Ramos and Joe Melig are offering barbacoa and similar dishes at their 2M Smokehouse.

Chefs who might have in the past opted to run fine dining establishments are opening barbecue joints instead. At Feges BBQ in Houston, both husband Patrick Feges and wife Erin Smith are classically trained chefs. She handles the sides while he takes care of the meats.

The contributions of African Americans to Texas barbecue past and present are being belatedly recognized. And while we're going back, we need to acknowledge that it was the Amerindians of the Caribbean who developed the technique for the slow, low cooking of meat indirectly over a framework of green wood. Spanish explorers observed the technique and named it *barbacoa*, the source of our English word *barbecue* and still the name for Mexican-influenced versions of the dish, especially around Texas today. Enslaved Africans brought the technique of slow, low cooking from West Africa too, and in places like Jamaica, the indigenous cooking styles and that of slaves and escaped slaves (Maroons) melded into the jerk tradition.

After introducing barbecue to the Deep South and then manning the pits, it was black slaves who familiarized Texas with barbecue in the nineteenth century.

Patillo's in Beaumont, the oldest African-American–owned barbecue restaurant in the state, founded in 1912, has probably gotten more ink in the last few years for its links than it has received in the rest of its history. Mary and Henry Gatlin, and their son Greg in Houston, are a great example of multiple generations working side by side to create some of the city's most respected Q, including extraordinary link sausage. Greg also runs Jackson Street BBQ with well-known chef Bryan Caswell and, among other things, serves a Sunday brunch with dishes like barbecued versions of deviled eggs and eggs Benedict, and a burnt ends sandwich on jalapeño cheese bread. Gatlin's links are USDA Prime brisket with loads of garlic and plenty of paprika for the perfect red grease stain, smoked over oak. Belender Wells and Alan Caldwell own Fargo's Pit BBQ in Bryan, and between the two of them, they do most every task.

The German, Polish, and Alsatian heritage of Central Texas has been well-documented as the source of the meat–market–style of barbecue, which typically includes smoking brisket, a cut that didn't have much interest to anyone otherwise, and making sausage to use up meat that hadn't sold. Cotton was the agricultural crop of note in the area. After slavery but before automated harvesting, migrant workers came to pick the crop. Cotton pickers in the early twentieth century needed food and would come into the meat markets to buy the barbecued meat. Because these were real markets, not restaurants, they had no plates, so the meat was served on sheets of butcher's paper. There were no conventional side dishes, so people would grab what they could—an onion, some bread, and maybe a hunk of cheese. That's part of the reason tradition holds that there's no sauce and no flatware. Southside Market in Elgin, originally downtown, has been selling its sausage since 1882. In Waco, Tony DeMaria's, started by an Italian family in the first half of the twentieth century, refers to its dipping sauce to this day as gravy, the term Italian-Americans use for marinara sauce.

"Barbecue was a shared tradition among slaves, and unlike the distinct regional 'cues we see today, the differences through the Antebellum South only hinged on what kind of wood and animal were available. So it's no surprise that we'd see cooking methods that were cemented in the plantations of Virginia, Georgia, and the Carolinas make their way into East Texas with the influx of slaves just before the Civil War."

—DANIEL VAUGHN,
TEXAS MONTHLY

The international influences continue to grow and evolve. In Austin at Kemuri Tatsu-ya, hip-hop DJs Tatsu Aikawa and Takuya "Tako" Matsumoto created a cross between a Japanese izakaya pub and a barbecue joint. Opened in 2017, Kemuri Tatsu-ya was recognized by Eater, *Bon Appétit*, and *GQ* as one of the country's best new restaurants. Ted's Farm BBQ, also in Austin, offers the Texas banh mi and rice bowl, with a choice of chopped barbecued brisket or pork belly or jalapeño-cheese sausage with the expected Vietnamese-style condiments. Barbecue legend Aaron Franklin and chef Tyson Cole, famed for his Uchi restaurants, have come up with Loro, an Asian smokehouse-bar. Graze at the bar on candied kettle corn with brisket burnt ends and togorashi Japanese seasoning or a pork sausage sandwich topped with papaya salad, Thai chile sauce, and peanuts. It's not all that different from a classic Southern sandwich with coleslaw and tangy red–chile–flecked sauce. In Houston, brothers Don and Theo Nguyen's Khoi Barbecue began with Central Texas–style brisket, but they have been adding more dishes from their family's heritage.

Women pitmasters and barbecue aficionados are putting their stamp on the field in important and more visible ways. Tootsie Tomanetz, now well into her eighties, oversees the pits at Snow's BBQ in Lexington along with owner Kerry Bexley. Miss Tootsie is out at those pits shoveling coals and shifting them and the meat around, but she always has time for the requested photos with her legion of fans. Mama Ernestine Edmonds owns Mama E's in Fort Worth and reigns as pitmaster there, having learned the barbecue craft at home as a child. Kim Dunn is the owner and pitmaster of Pit Stop Bar-B-Q in Temple. LeAnn Mueller runs Austin's wildly successful La Barbecue with her wife, Ali Clem. LeAnn is the granddaughter of Louie Mueller, whose namesake joint in Taylor won its own James Beard Foundation award as an America's Classic during her parents' stewardship and is now run by her brother Wayne. Ronda Richardson owns Doug's in Amarillo and has a woman pitmaster, Michelle Leach. Brett's Backyard Bar-B-Que in Rockdale has an entirely female crew of meat cutters. Jess Pryles, one of the state's top meat experts, created a line of Hardcore Carnivore rubs (my favorite is Black) and equipment available through jesspryles.com. She also designed a signature JP barbecue pit for Pitts & Spitts.

KEEPING THE FLAME

I hope this new collection of recipes and background will entertain you as well as encourage you to experiment in new ways. There's never been a more exciting time in the history of Texas Q. We can all be in the big tent of the barbecue community today. Come on in and let's get cooking.

CHAPTER 2

THE COMPLETE LONE STAR OUTDOOR KITCHEN: BARBECUE BASICS, FUELS, EQUIPMENT, AND TOOLS

Some pitmasters like to make novices think there's real magic behind methods, as if standing over some meat, scattering fairy dust, and whispering an incantation creates success. Actually, it's a bunch of incremental decisions—the food, the seasoning, the fuel, the equipment, time, temperature, and even your tools—that all contribute. Here's an overview of the items you might procure to help you succeed. The recipes that follow will guide you through everything else you need to know.

THE FOOD

Let's start at the start. The one thing that has improved barbecue substantially over recent years is the quality of the meat. Better quality going in makes better quality coming out. Today's beef, for example, is often grass-fed and finished and sometimes locally raised, and much of it is graded USDA Prime or high Choice. You'll now find branded beef, such as Certified Black Angus, which has to meet ten quality standards to get this designation. Other meats and poultry are being raised sustainably without hormones or antibiotics. Fruits and vegetables in side dishes are often now certified organic or at least pesticide- and herbicide-free. It's become much easier for home cooks to find these kinds of foods too, with the plethora of farmers markets, top

grocery chains, and butcher shops like Provision House in Dallas or Dai Due in Austin. Somewhat to the consternation of TSA, I even drag lard from Dai Due home to New Mexico because it's so well rendered.

Prices are higher for these foods, of course, and it follows that barbecue restaurants are charging more with the increase in quality. A single beef rib clocks in at $25, but you can just about feed a family on one of those. Barbecue is still one of the best food bargains you can enjoy when eating out and certainly when eating in.

Some of these meat cuts may need to be ordered ahead from your meat cutter or butcher or if you don't have one of those, a mail-order source. Here are a few family-run Lone Star sources of meats and other proteins:

44 Farms. This ranch produces premium (USDA Prime and high Choice) Black Angus grass-fed steaks, ground beef, and nitrate-free hot dogs. A good source for hefty bone-in beef plate short ribs (44Farms.com).

Broken Arrow Ranch. Mike Hughes started this south-central Texas company as a supplier of premium free-range venison such as axis deer and Nilgai antelope. Broken Arrow Ranch also offers wild boar, pasture-raised Dorper lamb, and Diamond H Ranch quail. You can also purchase a variety of raw and smoked game sausages, including venison bratwurst and venison-wild boar jalapeño-and-cheese links. Mike's son Chris

and Chris's wife, Maeve Hughes, now run the business (brokenarrowranch.com).

Prestige Oysters. Based in Dickinson, these folks ship sustainably raised Gulf oysters (prestigeoysters.com).

THE EQUIPMENT

I was reminded recently of something I wrote decades ago, in frustration over the lack of sources for equipment: ". . . shopping for a home smoker was akin to looking for a poker game in the Vatican. If you could find one at all, it was tucked away in a remote corner and no one in charge knew a thing about it." That's completely changed. All major big-box stores, hardware stores, sporting goods and outdoor outfitting stores, dedicated outdoor cooking stores, and even many kitchenware stores carry smokers in some form or another. Of course, you can find them all over the Internet, but if you have a local store selling what you want, I certainly recommend supporting your neighbors.

One of the characteristics to think about is whether you want a "stick burner," barbecue world lingo for a wood-burning pit, or a "gasser," a pit that uses gas for fuel and wood for flavoring, or other style of cooker.

THE MEDIUM IS THE MESSAGE— YOUR HEAT SOURCE FLAVORS THE FOOD

The best way to barbecue is with a log fire, which is how it all began. In the early years, the only equipment needed was an ax and a shovel. Prospective barbecuers cleared trees along a stretch of open land, cut the branches into logs, and loaded the wood into a long pit several feet deep. They burned the logs down to smoldering coals and cooked their food over the smoky fire for a full night or longer, adding wood as necessary to maintain a steady, low temperature.

The rich smokiness you want in all barbecue should come from smoldering wood, not from fat or oil dripping on coals or hot metal. The difference is enormous, both in taste and in health risk. The smoke produced by burning fat contains benzopyrene, a carcinogen that sticks to food. The effect is almost unavoidable in grilling, but it isn't a problem in barbecuing if you have a water reservoir or pan beneath the meat, an option with much of the equipment.

Whether you build or buy, your equipment is your key to barbecue success. You may be inclined after a while to give more credit to your skills and secret recipes, but you won't be bragging about much if you ever forget that the fire comes before the food. While everything you do makes some difference in your results, the most critical consideration is your smoking equipment and how you use it. A lot of devices will work, including homemade contraptions, inexpensive bullet (water) smokers, surefire metal pits, or even your old kettle grill. As long as you know your equipment and understand some barbecue basics, you're just a little practice short of your own bragging rights.

Barbecuing was the United States' original and most popular form of outdoor cooking until grilling surged into the forefront after the Second World War. Equipment was a major reason for the shift. By the 1950s, factories were turning out basic, cheap grills faster than Formica, but those who wanted a barbecue smoker for home use had to make it for themselves. That's still a good option for some people, even with the solid commercial products available today. A lot of barbecue cook-off champions work on homemade equipment, sometimes expensively fabricated pits in special shapes ranging from armadillos to whiskey bottles.

Homemade Smokers and Pits

Most do-it-yourselfers start with 55-gallon (208-L) metal drums—well-scrubbed ones that never contained anything toxic. They are moderately easy to convert into a smoker and, most important, they project an authentic homespun feel, letting everyone know you're danged serious.

A single drum cut in half horizontally, the most common design, is better for grilling than for smoking, but it can manage either. You split the barrel lengthwise, adding hinges on the back and a handle in front for a lid. Any kind of heavy metal grid can serve as a grate for holding the food. The most difficult part is attaching legs, usually accomplished by welding or bolting angle irons to the drum.

To avoid that job, you can use the barrel vertically, which elevates the working area to a comfortable height and also improves the smoke circulation needed for real barbecue. Among several options for rigging it, you can cut one end from the drum, place the opening over a brick fire pit, and hang meat from hooks secured to the vented top.

A double-barrel configuration is even better for barbecuing, though the construction is more complex. The bottom drum serves as an offset firebox, allowing you to keep the flame at an optimal distance from the food. Some experts recommend using parts from wood stoves for elements such as the firebox door, cast-iron supports, flues, and chimneys with dampers. Wood stove dealers and large hardware stores should have sources.

An experienced welder can build any of these barrel smokers, but a few tips may help you get it right. Remove any existing paint as well as you can and refinish all surfaces with a high-temperature paint. Install a good thermometer near the cooking area so you can check the temperature easily. Make sure you have a well-controlled flow of air from the firebox, across the food, and out through a chimney or vent at the opposite end of the smoker. A baffle may help ensure proper smoke circulation. To cook with logs instead of charcoal, line the bottom of the barrel with sand and firebrick to keep the wood from burning through and to reinforce the heat-retention properties of the thin metal.

A brick pit is another option for anyone with a lifetime address and basic masonry skills. A simple brick rectangle with a metal grate and lid will work, though it's better to add an attached outside firebox at one end of the pit and a chimney at the other, both fitted with mechanisms for regulating air circulation. Even someone like me, who isn't handy at all, can make a temporary version of a similar pit. Just stack concrete blocks about 3 feet (0.9 m) high in a cleared, level area—perhaps a driveway—borrow a grate from your grill or oven, and use heavy-duty aluminum foil as a lid.

What you can barbecue well depends on what you build. A double-barrel pit or a sophisticated brick pit have the same kind of broad range as a store-bought log-burner. Other homemade options are more limited in capabilities, but any that can handle a true wood fire have more potential than a manufactured charcoal smoker.

It's the Pits!

Barbecue pits, trenches or holes really, originally were open on top, with the meat hung above the fire or placed on a ground-level grate. Sheet metal might cover it, with dirt thrown over it to keep the heat in. At what's called the World's Largest Free Barbecue, or just "The Feed," at the XIT Rodeo and Reunion in Dalhart each August, that's still the way almost 10,000 pounds (4,536 kg) of beef shoulder clod is cooked.

Many people still barbecue in a similar style, and I describe how to cook that way later in this chapter. Around the beginning of the twentieth century, though, the state's first commercial barbecue joints introduced important changes in the technology.

Much of the credit goes to immigrant German butchers, who initially knew little about American barbecue but a great deal about old-country methods of smoking sausage and pork. In meat markets, they introduced Texans to the European art of charcuterie and learned in turn from their customers about American smoked meats. The two traditions merged easily in places such as the Kreuz Market in Lockhart, Texas, where the butchers built a large brick pit in the back of the shop to smoke all kinds of fare. For barbecuing, the pit offered many advantages over an open underground trench. The brick walls elevated the working level enough to keep the cooks out of the chiropractor's office, and the newfangled metal lid trapped heat and smoke inside to make the cooking process more efficient and even. The homespun inventors also placed the fire farther from the food, often moving the burning logs from directly underneath the meat to the far end of the long pit opposite an outside vent.

Hundreds of other barbecuers created their own similar closed pits, simple but ingenious contraptions that carried an old legacy into a new age. No one has really improved on the design in the century since, and in recent decades, it has become the model for a big breakthrough in home barbecue equipment.

Starting around 1980, several small but dynamic companies began manufacturing log-burning metal pits. Many of them had an offset firebox at one end and a chimney at the other, just like that ancient brick pit at Kreuz Market, but some were more vertical in shape, with the wood

directly under the food. In either case, the basic design was borrowed from oil drums and other oil-field equipment. All of these smokers keep the fire well away from the meat, get good smoke circulation, and maintain a constant low temperature for extended periods, regulating the heat with damper controls. You check the temperature every twenty to thirty minutes and add wood as needed, maybe once an hour.

The advantage of burning logs is the density of wood smoke they produce. Like the lava rocks in a gas or electrical grill, most charcoal doesn't generate smoke unless fat or food falls on it. So a major part of the heat source in any kind of charcoal, gas, or electrical device cooks food without smoking it, regardless of how many wood chips or chunks you use. You can barbecue many things well with this kind of equipment, as my recipes show, but you can never quite match the smokiness of the brisket at a great barbecue joint.

Moberg Smokers, welder Sunny Moberg's custom company out of Dripping Springs, builds pits for some of the biggest names in commercial barbecue. His operation has skyrocketed in recognition and popularity as the demand for high-quality equipment has increased exponentially in the last decade. The wait for his custom rigs has been hefty, but he's been in expansion mode, so hopefully you can take delivery on one ordered while you're still young enough to cook Q (moberg-smokers.com). Houston-based Gator Pit of Texas (gatorpit.net) makes high-quality handcrafted custom pits and barbecue trailers. Owner Ritch Robin conjured up a 13-foot (4 m)–long "Space Shuttle BBQ Pit" for an important exhibition in 2018 to 2019 called Barbecue Nation, which was put together through the Atlanta History Center. East Texas Smoker Company in Tyler also makes some very fine handcrafted custom pits and barbecue trailers (easttexassmokercompany.com). For commercial use, J&R Manufacturing in

Mesquite offers the cabinet smoker called The Oyler Pit, with its well-liked wood-fired rotisserie, along with models such as The Little Red Smokehouse and Smokemaster Convection Oven. Even if you're not in market for commercial equipment, it's worth reading about their models for features you might want to look for in a backyard smoker.

PRIME LOG-BURNING PITS

Top-of-the-line log pits produce those fully flavored traditional barbecue meats, and they do it to perfection. If you are set on making the best beef brisket or shoulder clod in town, this is the way to go. The premier pits, called Texas hibachis by some wags, are made by custom fabricators, weigh several hundred pounds, and cost in the same range as a high-quality gas grill. The weight and expense come from the use of thick, heavy-gauge metal that's capable of standing up to serious log fires for a lifetime of use.

If you read chapter 1, you know how a Pitts & Spitts pit adopted my husband and me back in the 1990s. It's one of the Houston company's moderate-size models. While the company changed hands some years ago, the craftsmanship on all their products continues to be outstanding in looks, durability, and capability. The pits feature an offset firebox with ¼-inch (6-mm) plate walls, marine-grade stainless steel parts, an accurate industrial thermometer, a water reservoir with a drain, and superior smoke drafting. Visit the virtual showroom at pittsandspitts.com. Many other companies make pits throughout Texas, including Texas Original Pits (texasoriginalpits.com), Big Hat Bar-B-Q (bighatbbq.com), BBQ Pits by Klose (bbqpits.net), and Lang BBQ Smokers (langbbqsmokers.com). Respected pitmasters are getting into the smoker business too. Arnis Robbins of Evie Mae's Pit Barbecue in

Wolfforth makes EM Smokers, ranging from patio size to 10,000-gallon (38-kl) trailer models (eviemaesbbq.com). About the time this book was going to press, Aaron Franklin was ready to launch his own line of backyard smokers from Franklin Barbecue Pits (franklinbbqpits.com).

When you compare the range of choices among companies' models, be sure to look at all the features, not just the cost. Consider the heft of the firebox and the lightness of the lid. Decide the value of a water reservoir, which helps keep meat juicy and eliminates the possible carcinogenic effects of fat dripping on hot metal. Examine the quality of the metal fabrication, even the sturdiness of the wheels. All the details matter, because a prime log pit should provide a lifetime of barbecue bliss.

"This is trial by fire It's a post-oak fueled gauntlet that would cause most of us to fold faster than a lawn chair in a windstorm. But these few aren't most of us. They're pitmasters. Smoke charmers . . . These . . . are the ladies and gentlemen who tease flavor out of trees . . ."

—YETI AD,
2017

POPULAR VALUE PITS

One of the few liabilities of the top log pits is their size. The heavy-duty construction is an asset in barbecuing, but it makes the pits fairly expensive and bulky. If your bank account or outdoor space is limited, you might want to look at other ways to cook with wood.

The best alternatives are the moderately priced, lighter-weight pits that are becoming widely available in warehouse clubs and large hardware shops. They look similar to their big brothers and function much the same, but the thinner metal of the firebox is more suitable for wood chunks than large logs. What you sacrifice in capability and features, you make up for in savings. Regular retail prices start around $300, and you can find bargains for less.

For all kinds of pit smokers, the fullest list of fabricators that I've found is at Jeff Phillips's forum: smokingmeatforums.com/a/smoker-man ufacturer-list.8611

Outdoor Ovens

Another good option for barbecuing is a smoker oven. They generally produce less smoky flavor than a log or chunk pit, but they are easy and economical to use. Cookshack (cookshack.com), out of Oklahoma, makes one I have used for a couple of decades. Primarily a manufacturer of commercial barbecue equipment, the company also offers a model suitable for home use that operates just like the bigger restaurant ones. Powered by electricity, it burns wood chunks in a tightly sealed oven that you turn on and don't touch again until you're done.

Traeger Pellet Grills (traegergrills.com) have come to dominate the pellet grill market. You set the grill at an appropriate smoking temperature and load a supply of wood pellets, available in many woods and flavorings. A patented auger mechanism feeds the wood into a small, efficient firebox under the cooking grate. Bradley Smoker (bradleysmoker.com) sells an oven that looks similar but operates a little differently. An electrically powered smoke generator burns special "Bradley Flavour Bisquettes," compressed hardwood chips about the size of a hockey puck. An automatic mechanism feeds the fire as needed with new bisquettes, which are produced from a variety of woods such as alder, apple, and hickory. Yoder, made in Kansas City, has pellet cookers that have been great for smoking and baking but couldn't get the direct heat needed for grilling. More recently it has added a package to its YS series that works great according to friends who wanted that capability too. (Yoder also makes a high-quality offset-firebox log-burning pit.) Even Texas barbecue pit heavyweight Pitts & Spitts makes a pellet smoker/grill. Also take a look at REC TEC pellet smokers. They have all the bells and whistles with Wi-Fi and phone apps, but I most like that the pellet hopper can hold up to 40 pounds (18 kg) of pellets. You could probably barbecue an elephant (just kidding!) before you'd need to add wood.

All of these smokers are distinctive additions to the patio, marking you as a special kind of outdoor cook, but none of them compare in individuality to the Big Green Egg (biggreenegg. com). A charcoal smoker and grill, it's modeled on the Japanese kamado, a clay oven that looks like an oversized egg. The thick ceramic walls efficiently retain heat and moisture, keeping food naturally juicy without the use of a water pan. It's my all-time favorite piece of equipment for moist, smoky chicken with crackling crisp skin.

The grill-style oven that I use the most is the Hasty-Bake (hastybake.com). In business since 1948, Hasty-Bake has legions of dedicated fans, just like the Big Green Egg's eggers. Fired by charcoal, it's equally adept as a grill and a smoker, which isn't always the case with products that claim both capabilities. The flexibility comes from an adjustable firebox and a side door for loading fuel. You can regulate the temperature by raising or lowering the firebox, and you can add charcoal and wood without opening the lid and releasing heat.

Charcoal and Gas Grills

You can also barbecue in many conventional grills that lack an adjustable firebox. The challenge is greater because it's more difficult to maintain constant low temperatures long enough to get the right result. Some grills manage that task better than others. Check out the capabilities of your grill by starting with foods that require relatively short smoking times, such as boneless chicken breasts, fish, and vegetables.

A grill cover is necessary for smoking, along with an ample supply of wood chips and chunks. The rest is straightforward, if not simple. On the most common grills, you cook with indirect heat by placing the food over a pan of water on the opposite side of the grill from the fire and wood. Consult the owner's manual for specific indirect cooking instructions for your grill.

The key to success is a low cooking temperature. That's easier to attain initially with charcoal grills but easier to maintain during a slow cooking process with gas grills. If your charcoal grill has vents, as many popular models do, close them most of the way to hold down the intensity of the fire, and try not to lift the lid except to add more wood or charcoal. Many gas grills are limited in their range of cooking temperatures and simply won't go low enough for real barbecuing, but when they do, they hold a steady heat level with less fuss. I use my Ducane gas grill frequently for barbecuing ribs, pork steaks, or smaller foods.

Bullet Smokers

Bullet smokers, also called water smokers or vertical smokers, are most folks' entry-level dedicated smoker. They appear in almost every store that sells outdoor products. They deserve their popularity in many respects, providing a solid combination of value, versatility, ease, and efficiency. The market is dominated today by Weber's Smokey Mountain. Starting well below $100, they are relatively simple to use, require minimal attention during operation, and yield fine results with many foods, particularly items that benefit from a moist cooking process. The most serious shortcoming is with traditional barbecue meats such beef brisket and pork shoulder, which remain excessively fatty because of the added moisture.

All bullet smokers look much the same and operate on similar principles. Shaped like *Star Wars*' beloved R2-D2, they have a domed lid (often fitted with an imprecise thermometer), one or two grates for food, a pan for holding water or other liquids, and a charcoal, electric, or gas heat source on the bottom. The water helps keep the temperature low and prevents the undesirable smoke produced by fat falling in the fire. It also adds considerable moistness to food, much more than you get from a water reservoir in a log pit. When you want a crisp, crunchy finish in a dish, you can cook without the water pan or remove the pan during the last stages of cooking.

Among the various models, the electric versions are the most reliable and convenient, at least if you have a handy power outlet. They cost more initially than their charcoal counterparts, but the fuel is much cheaper over time. Their primary advantage is a steady, dependable cooking temperature. The temperature will vary a little between different smokers and climates and will drop some in cold weather or when you're using an extension cord, but it does remain fairly

constant during the cooking process on any particular day. Gas water smokers share that strength, but they get pricey and aren't as widely available.

Charcoal models fluctuate in cooking temperature, following a standard bell curve. They fire up gradually, reach a peak temperature that can approach 300°F (150°C) when the coals are at their hottest, and then drop steadily as the charcoal dies down. You can mitigate the effect by lighting only a small circle of coals in the center and allowing them to ignite the others over time, but you still get temperature variations. You have to rely on the average heat level, which can be difficult to determine accurately, to estimate the cooking time required for a dish. Compounding this potential problem, weather variables such as cold and wind affect the temperature more in charcoal smokers than in electric ones, and they take longer to regain heat any time you lift the lid. With a little experience, the cooking process becomes easy, but I found this highly frustrating at first. They cost little to buy, but remember that you'll be going through substantial amounts of charcoal with every cook.

FUELS

Cigars produce smoke and so does burning fat, but you don't want to cook with either one. The smoke flavor in real barbecue should come mainly from wood. If you aren't using it in one form or another, you aren't barbecuing. You need a fire that creates that holy grail for great flavor: blue smoke, not a billowing cloud of white or gray.

Only hardwoods work. Soft, resinous woods like pine or cedar contain too much sap, which makes their smoke harsh and foul-tasting. Avoid plywood, construction scraps, or anything you cannot positively identify as an appropriate untreated hardwood.

Much has been written of the woods for Texas barbecue, and it used to be easy to chart where you were in the state by the aroma of the smoke. Hickory was East Texas, mesquite was West, and in between in Central Texas and the Hill Country, it was oak, post oak as well as some live oak or red oak. Pecan appeared here and there. While there was plenty of jawboning about which wood was best, it pretty much boiled down to what trees grew in your neck of the woods. These days, wood, whether logs, chunks, chips, or pellets, is hauled all over and mixed and matched as creative cooks wish. If you need to order, try Western Premium BBQ Products in Pleasanton for chips, chunks, and logs (westernbbqproducts.com). Their packaged wood can be found in many Texas supermarkets and sporting goods stores too.

As much attention as is devoted to this topic of which wood to use, it's actually probably more important that you use seasoned wood. Freshly chopped wood has a moisture content of about 50 percent. Seasoned wood has been given time to dry so that both moisture and sap from the tree have evaporated. It should have a silver-gray cast to it, no matter what kind of wood it is. Also, the wood will likely be developing noticeable cracks and the bark will be loose. Split wood rather than whole logs will lose moisture more quickly. If in doubt, a moisture meter from a hardware store can rate the moisture content, which typically should register between 9 and 15 percent. (I found out these moisture meters also come in handy when you have a leak in your roof that seeps down into your wall.)

If you will be burning a combination of wood and charcoal, Jeddo-based company B & B Charcoal Factory (bbcharcoal.com) makes an array of products including charcoal briquettes, hardwood lump charcoal, and char-logs. They offer pellets and kiln-dried smallish logs too.

TOOLS AND EQUIPMENT

Cooler. Yeti, the Austin-based company that makes high-end ice chests, coolers, and insulated drinkware, is a common presence at barbecue and related events around the state. The ice chests are so good at insulating that you can use them to keep food hot too, for finishing briskets, ribs, and other serious meat wrapped in butcher paper. If you want to use them for cooling, I recently hosted a party where I had my Yeti cooler holding supplemental iced-down drinks. After the event, I didn't realize for four days that it hadn't been cleaned out that night. When I opened the cooler, it was still full of ice and cold drinks and felt like a rush of air conditioning in my toasty July kitchen. Like a high-end barbecue pit, Yeti equipment should be considered a lifetime investment, well worth the money if it's a priority to you (yeti.com). I love their new purple!

Burn barrel or box. My friend, cowboy cook and pitmaster Tom Perini of the Perini Ranch Steakhouse, taught me how to use burn barrels or boxes. When Tom and his wife, Lisa, smoke beef or pork at their restaurant or for caterings, they have a big lineup of these 55-gallon (208 L) metal drums for continuously cooking logs down to coals. Tom's crew uses the barrels laid on their sides, but some people fashion them to stand upright. In either case, as coals are ready, they are shoveled into the smoker for cooking. I like this technique for mesquite in particular because the smoke from burning logs can become somewhat acrid during the long cooking needed for barbecue. It's still a distinctive smoke, but the bitter edge disappears when using coals rather than logs.

Here are some other things you may want or need:

Instant-read thermometer. The Yeti of thermometers is the Thermapen from Thermoworks (thermoworks.com). It'll change your life. If you don't believe me, that's pretty much what the food-nerd folks at America's Test Kitchen think too.

Fire starters. For wood fires, I use Weber's widely available paraffin lighter cubes. They can be used to fire up charcoal too, but for that, I prefer to use a charcoal chimney. Fatwood sticks, readily found in hardware stores or from L.L.Bean online, can be used too.

Extension cords for electric equipment. Get ones intended for heavy-duty use—3-prong 10-amp, 12-gauge.

Silicone brushes. I still have a couple of small string mops used by barbecuers in days past for old time's sake, but I've mostly switched over to silicone brushes. You can find all sizes, so get a variety. They're so easy to clean by running through the dishwasher.

Tongs. I have always hated anything packaged as barbecue tools—the oversize forks, knives, spatulas. They are typically clunky, heavy, and scaled for the Incredible Hulk. Get yourself a couple pairs of quality tongs. I like the OXO brand because of their size but also because they have silicone inserts down the sides that keep hands from being easily burned.

Offset spatula. Get a decent size and weight pancake turner. The handle doesn't need to be huge, just sturdy.

Neoprene, silicone, or suede gloves. You'll want to be able to move hot equipment and hot food (jesspryles.com).

Bear Paws. I'm not big on gadgets, but these work for multiple tasks. Sometimes called bear claws, these are plastic paws or claws that are meant for shredding pork and other meats. They are really handy for lifting turkey breasts or other large pieces of meat. Get a dishwasher-safe plastic set of them from Amazon for less than a barbecue sandwich typically costs.

Drip pan. Different than a water pan, you want something that fits under food that is likely to drip delectable juices. You may want to put a bit of stock or water in it to start so that the drippings don't burn before they have accumulated. Foil pans work fine for this purpose.

Bleach. For cleanup, use 1 tablespoon (15 ml) of bleach in a gallon (3.8 L) of water. This is especially handy if you're some distance from a real kitchen with running hot water.

Books. Every ten to twelve minutes, the time it takes to grill a chicken breast, another book that purports to teach you about barbecue—real barbecue—hits the market. I buy lots of them since I'm passionate about the craft. However, beyond my own classic *Smoke & Spice*, I recommend three other terrific books I consider essential. Meathead Goldwyn's book *Meathead* goes into the science of why various cooking techniques and equipment work—or don't—and he breaks it all down in a fun and accessible way. You can always go to his website, amazingribs.com, for information too, but as an author, I like to encourage people to pay for the work of other authors. Aaron Franklin's *Franklin Barbecue: A Meat-Smoking Manifesto* is just that. It's devoted to telling you his story and laying out, with great generosity, everything he does to smoke the ultimate Texas brisket so that you can too. For a real flavor of Texas barbecue, I love Robb Walsh's *Legends of Texas Barbecue Cookbook*, the smoke-filled history of Lone Star barbecue culture. If you have more room in your library, add in Daniel Vaughn's *The Prophets of Smoked Meat: A Journey Through Texas Barbecue* and photographer Wyatt McSpadden's two volumes, *Texas BBQ* and *Texas BBQ: Small Town to Downtown*. None of these last three will make you a better cook, at least directly, but they offer great inspiration about the heritage of barbecue, as well as where it is today and where to head out to sample it. The more inspired and curious you are, the better cook I think you will become.

REALLY
SMOKING

CHAPTER 3

LONE STAR RUBS AND SEASONINGS

**W**hen I first wrote about barbecue, lots of people didn't understand what a dry rub was. I can remember demonstrating time and again how you would really rub a good quantity of these seasoning blends into the surface of your food, not just sprinkle a bit over like you might paprika on a deviled egg. Seasoning mixtures can take the form of dry rubs, wet marinades, or a paste of herbs with garlic or onion and some oil, but for most serious Texas Q, you want to stay dry. A few more seasonings are included in the recipe section, ones that go best with a particular dish but without as broad an appeal as those here. While your barbecue cooks, you may want to use a liquid to help keep it moist. That's where a mop comes in. Through judicious use of layers of flavor paired with smoke, you create the ultimate barbecue.

Slather It On

Lots of pitmasters and other barbecue cooks like to slather their meat or other protein in something that will stick firmly to the surface and also will help hold a dry rub on securely. The slather can help create a tender bark that still has a good chew to it. I don't always find it a necessity, but I do like to use the technique on leaner cuts like bison or pork tenderloin. Mustard, usually the yellow variety, is a popular choice, especially mixed with some dill pickle juice. Sometimes, I use soy sauce with a little Chinese oyster sauce mixed in for thickness and that deep umami quality. Mayonnaise can be used too, maybe with some chili powder mixed in. Or, mix up a combination that appeals to you. Savory Spice Shop (savoryspiceshop.com) carries a lot of barbecue-related products, including 'Cue Glue, which is a handy variation on the mustard-and-pickle-juice theme.

You might think that a combination of these two seasonings sounds duller than a butter knife. There's a reason, though, that in centuries past, battles have been fought and trade routes established over these now-familiar, always-available staples. Few spices amp up the inherent flavor of food better than salt and pepper, and using a coarse-ground variety of each gives some desirable texture on a barbecued food's surface too. Dalmatian's the choice of many a pitmaster. I sometimes build on this with a couple of tablespoons of (11 g) cayenne, (20 g) granulated garlic, or a dried herb such as (6 g) oregano mixed in.

DALMATIAN RUB: ELEMENTAL SALT AND PEPPER

PREPARATION TIME: LESS THAN 5 MINUTES

MAKES ABOUT 1½ CUPS (250 G)

1 cup (96 g) coarsely ground or cracked black pepper
½ cup (150 g) kosher salt or coarse sea salt

Mix the black pepper and salt thoroughly in a bowl. Store covered in a cool, dark pantry.

VARIATION: Smoky Salt and Pepper. *Add smoke to either the salt or the pepper. You don't need to do both. When you're planning to smoke any other dish, pour a thin layer of either salt or black pepper into a shallow pan or tray. Place the pan in the smoker in a spot where juices from any other food can't drip into the pan. Smoke 20 to 30 minutes. Stir together with whichever ingredient you didn't smoke and store covered in a cool, dark pantry.*

Forgive me a little reminiscing. This was my late husband Bill's all-purpose rub, relied on for stellar brisket but also chicken, pork, and even smoked cheese. If we had ever decided to get into selling dry rubs, this would have been our initial launch. So many people have commented on their continued use of this Texas-inspired blend from Smoke & Spice *that I felt the need to reprint it here for newer audiences. Make a big batch so you always have it on hand.*

WILD WILLY'S NUMBER ONE-DERFUL RUB

PREPARATION TIME: 5 MINUTES

MAKES ABOUT 2 CUPS (280 G)

¾ cup (84 g) sweet paprika or Spanish smoked sweet paprika
¼ cup (24 g) coarse-ground black pepper
¼ cup (75 g) kosher salt or coarse sea salt
¼ cup (50 g) sugar
2 tablespoons (15 g) chili powder (Bill preferred Gebhardt's)
2 tablespoons (18 g) garlic powder
2 tablespoons (14 g) onion powder
2 teaspoons ground cayenne

Mix the paprika, black pepper, salt, sugar, chili powder, garlic powder, onion powder, and cayenne thoroughly in a bowl. Store covered in a cool, dark pantry.

The red of the paprika along with ruddy Worcestershire powder enhances the color of ribs or other lighter-colored fare. The Worcestershire powder adds powerful flavor to dry rubs and lets you put a serious crust on those ribs or even a burger. I get this dehydrated version of Worcestershire sauce from Fort Worth–based spice purveyor Pendery's (penderys.com).

RED DIRT

PREPARATION TIME: LESS THAN
5 MINUTES

MAKES ABOUT ¾ CUP (120 G)

½ cup (72 g) Worcestershire powder

2 tablespoons (14 g) smoked paprika

2 tablespoons (12 g) finely ground
   black pepper

1 tablespoon (19 g) kosher salt
   or coarse sea salt

Mix the Worcestershire powder, paprika, black pepper, and salt thoroughly in a bowl. Store covered in a cool, dark pantry.

A Dandy and His Dandy Spice Blends
In 1870, DeWitt Clinton Pendery alighted from a horse-drawn stagecoach with a waxed mustache, morning coat, and silk top hat in rough-and-tumble Fort Worth. He managed to survive taunts and tussles to thrive as a merchant. By the late 1800s, he was selling his line of seasonings inspired by his new residence to restaurants, hotels, and locals. He was among the first Texas shopkeepers to develop and sell a chili powder blend, which he promoted for its healthful properties as well as good taste. That and just about any other spice or seasoning blend you might want is available from Pendery's, still based in Fort Worth.

Here's a more richly favored chili powder than you find in your average grocery store.

CHILE DUST

PREPARATION TIME: 5 MINUTES

MAKES ABOUT ½ CUP (80 G)

¼ cup (30 g) ancho chile powder

2 tablespoons (15 g) guajillo chile
   powder or New Mexican dried
   red chile powder

1½ tablespoons (28 g) kosher salt or
   coarse sea salt

2 teaspoons onion powder

1 teaspoon garlic powder

½ teaspoon ground cumin

Mix the ancho chile, guajillo chile, salt, onion powder, garlic powder, and cumin thoroughly in a bowl. Store covered in a cool, dark pantry.

Texas Born and Bred

There's agreement that chili powder, the blend of ground chile and other seasonings that gives Tex-Mex foods their signature flavor profile, was born in Texas. It saved the cook, whether in a home kitchen or bustling restaurant galley, from needing to dry and pulverize chile pods and blend them with cumin seeds and other seasonings. One camp, including chili aficionado Joe Cooper, claims the mixture was invented by German immigrant William Gebhardt. His spice-grinding process was inspired by the technique used for preparing Hungarian paprika in the Old Country.

I tend to keep the rubs for beef pretty simple these days, but I love a bit more complexity for pork, especially brown sugar and the added sweetness of paprika and the more astringent quality of dry mustard. Adjust as you like though.

PORK RIB AND BELLY RUB

PREPARATION TIME: 5 MINUTES

MAKES ABOUT 1½ CUPS (260 G)

½ cup (115 g) packed dark brown sugar
½ cup (56 g) sweet paprika
2 tablespoons (18 g) dry mustard
2 tablespoons (14 g) onion powder
2 tablespoons (38 g) kosher salt or coarse sea salt
1 tablespoon (19 g) hickory-smoked salt
   (or additional kosher salt or coarse sea salt)
2 teaspoons ground *chile pequin* or cayenne

Mix the spices thoroughly in a bowl. Store covered in a cool, dark pantry.

This will wake up your mouth. Grind the coffee just before putting this together for the best jolt of flavor. This rub is perfect for pork, but if you want to use on beef, reduce the sugar by 2 tablespoons (30 g).

JOLT

PREPARATION TIME: 5 MINUTES

MAKES ABOUT 1 CUP (140 G)

½ cup (28 g) finely ground coffee
¼ cup (60 g) packed light or dark brown sugar
2 tablespoons (38 g) kosher salt or coarse sea salt
2 tablespoons (12 g) ground black pepper
1 teaspoon ground cayenne

Mix the coffee, brown sugar, salt, black pepper, and cayenne thoroughly in a bowl. Store in a cool, dark pantry.

The Open Secret
One of the steadfast marinades for Texas barbecue, especially chicken and fajitas, remains Wish-Bone Italian salad dressing. Whether a home cook or competition cook, additional Italian dressing may serve as the mop or baste too.

This was the first mop I learned to use, and it still holds up on briskets, beef ribs, pork ribs, and just about anything else.

BEER MOP FOR BEEF AND JUST ABOUT EVERYTHING

PREPARATION TIME: 5 MINUTES

COOKING TIME: 5 MINUTES

MAKES ABOUT 4 CUPS (946 ML)

12 ounces (355 ml) beer, preferably
   medium-bodied
1 cup (235 ml) water
½ cup (120 ml) cider vinegar
¼ cup (60 ml) vegetable oil
½ medium onion, chopped or sliced
   into thin rings
1 fresh or pickled jalapeño pepper,
   sliced thinly, optional
1 tablespoon (15 ml)
   Worcestershire sauce
1 tablespoon (10 g) whatever dry rub
   is being used to flavor the food
   (optional)

Combine the beer, water, vinegar, oil, onion, jalapeño, Worcestershire sauce, and dry rub in a saucepan. Warm the mop over medium heat, bringing it just to a boil. Lower the heat and keep the mixture warm over low heat, adding water if it reduces so much that it can't be drizzled easily.

Some of the earliest seasonings for Texas barbecue were remarkably similar to those elsewhere in the country, often a liquid that was more mop than sauce. Butter, lard, or beef tallow was mixed with some vinegar and salt and pepper. The mixtures have gotten more elaborate as condiments have grown exponentially and barbecuers have sought to set their Q apart from others.

MUSTARD MOP FOR PORK AND CHICKEN

PREPARATION TIME: 5 MINUTES

COOKING TIME: 5 MINUTES

MAKES ABOUT 4 CUPS (946 ML)

3 cups (700 ml) water

1 large onion, chopped or sliced into thin rings

4 tablespoons (55 g) salted butter

3 tablespoons (45 ml) Worcestershire sauce

2 tablespoons (18 g) dry mustard

1 tablespoon (10 g) of the dry rub used to flavor your food (optional)

Combine the ingredients in a saucepan. Warm the mop over medium heat, just to a boil. Keep the mixture warm over low heat, adding water if it reduces so much that it can't be drizzled easily.

VARIATION: Citrus-Mustard Mop for Beef, Pork, and Chicken. *Reduce the Worcestershire sauce by 1 tablespoon (15 ml). Add the juice of a couple of halved lemons and toss in the juiced lemon peels too. OR use ½ to 1 cup (120 to 235 ml) orange juice, fresh or from concentrate, and 1 small sliced orange to the pan. Heat as above.*

The tang of vinegar makes the perfect foil for rich meats like pork ribs or butt or beef cheeks or brisket. You will want a spray bottle for this so you can spritz it over the smoking food rather than mopping or drizzling it over. If you like the idea of a little extra zip in your spritz, you can add a little Worcestershire sauce, fish sauce, or hot sauce. Just don't add anything that won't spray through the fine nozzle.

VINEGAR SPRITZ

PREPARATION TIME: LESS THAN 5 MINUTES

MAKES ABOUT 2 CUPS (475 ML)

2 cups (475 ml) white or cider vinegar

2 teaspoons Worcestershire sauce, fish sauce, or hot sauce (optional)

Pour the vinegar and sauce, if using, into a spray bottle. Spritz over your food about once an hour or as you wish while barbecuing.

"[Barbecue sauce] is made simply of vinegar and hot water, melted butter if the purse allows, or rendered beef suet if not, black and red pepper and salt (pioneer sauce stopped there) and generous dashes of catsup and Worcestershire sauce. Onions and sometimes lemons are sliced into it . . ."

DALLAS MORNING NEWS,
MARCH 26, 1937

My Appropriated Secret
Fish sauce adds plenty of character to beef, chicken, fish, and more. It's a little stinky if you're not used to it, but it leaves a nice elusive taste with a good amount of saltiness. I sometimes mix it with a little vinegar or lime juice for chicken in particular.

CHAPTER 4

PARTY STARTERS AND WHILE-YOU-WAIT SNACKS

**W**hen you're barbecuing to kick off football season via TV or stadium tailgating, celebrating a day at the lake, or simply inviting the neighborhood over for your bigger barbecued treats, you need a solid collection of smoked little nibbles. Whether you prefer melting cheese, seafood, wings, or serious meat, there's something here in this condensed collection of every style. These are all designed to fit on the pit for a brief time while you have a longer smoking project underway. Depending on the ease and speed of firing up your smoker though, you might want to cook up a few of them for an appetizer spread. In that case, I'd recommend adding a couple of non-smoked things, maybe as simple as some crisp vegetables and dip or some guacamole and chips. Party on!

"Pickles, Texas Toast & Apricots
are served at your request."

—MENU AT SUTPHEN'S BBQ,
BORGER, TEXAS

Perhaps the best snack ever while barbecuing is queso. The cooking temperature's a little flexible, which means you can place the cheese in the smoker with a variety of other foods. I wouldn't fire up a wood-burning pit just to add smoke to some melty cheese, but if it's going already, you bet. I certainly can see plugging in an electric smoker or whipping out my stovetop smoker to prepare this as an appetizer. You do want to keep the cheese in one or two large chunks, which keeps it from melting too quickly before picking up some good smoke. You have the option of adding a little more smoke with a slug of mezcal. Technically, this is more of a queso fundido, *or simply melted cheese. Whatever you call it, don't miss out on it.*

SMOKIN' QUESO

PREPARATION TIME: ABOUT
5 MINUTES

COOKING TIME: ABOUT 30 MINUTES

MAKES ABOUT 2 CUPS (475 ML)

12 ounces (340 g) medium Cheddar
   cheese, or half Cheddar and
   half Monterey Jack or pepper
   Jack cheese
1 or 2 pickled or fresh jalapeños,
   sliced
1 tablespoon (15 ml) mezcal
   (optional)
Tortilla chips or warm flour tortillas,
   for serving

1   Prepare the smoker for barbecuing, bringing the temperature to 225°F to 275°F (107°C to 140°C).

2   Place the cheese in a small cast-iron skillet or smokeproof baking dish. Scatter the jalapeños over the cheese to taste. Spoon the mezcal over the cheese, if using.

3   Place the cheese in the smoker, as far from the heat source as possible. Cook until the cheese melts thoroughly, about 30 to 35 minutes. Avoid overcooking once melted because the cheese will become rubbery.

4   Serve immediately, spooning the queso out onto tortilla chips or warm tortillas.

Perhaps the only thing that can improve on the elemental jalapeño popper is to add barbecued brisket to it.

BRISKET-STUFFED JALAPEÑO POPPERS

PREPARATION TIME: 15 MINUTES

COOKING TIME: ABOUT 30 MINUTES

MAKES 24 POPPERS

4 ounces (115 g) cream cheese,
  softened
4 ounces (115 g) mild or medium
  Cheddar cheese, shredded
Heaping ½ cup (113 g) shredded
  smoked brisket
12 medium to large fresh jalapeños,
  halved lengthwise, stems and
  seeds removed
6 thin slices uncooked bacon

1   Prepare the smoker for barbecuing, bringing the temperature to 225°F (107°C).

2   Combine the cream cheese, Cheddar, and brisket in a small bowl. Spoon the mixture into the jalapeño halves, mounding it up in the center of each.

3   Cut the bacon slices in half horizontally and wrap a half slice lengthwise around each pepper half. Secure with a toothpick. Arrange the jalapeños in a shallow smokeproof dish or on a piece of heavy-duty foil molded into a small tray.

4   Place the dish in the smoker and cook until the bacon has browned and crisped and the cheese is gooey, about 30 minutes. Serve right away.

Smoked
You can smoke so many things when your cooker is already fired up—potato chips, tortilla chips, olives, salt, pepper, deviled eggs, tomatoes, onions, salad dressing, vinegar, soy sauce, you name it. You might want to skip the raisin bran, but briefly smoking cereal such as Chex before adding it to party mix is pretty darned inspired.

Canned tuna pureed with liquid smoke recipes abound, but here's how you really should make the Gulf Coast's favorite sunset nibble. Even if you normally prefer tuna steaks cooked very rare, the texture of this dip is best if the fish is fully—if barely—cooked through. A somewhat thin steak will absorb more smoke.

PORT ARANSAS TUNA DIP

PREPARATION TIME: 15 MINUTES, PLUS 1 HOUR'S REFRIGERATION

COOKING TIME: ABOUT 45 MINUTES

MAKES ABOUT 2 CUPS (475 ML)

1 (8- to 10-ounce [225- to 280-g]) tuna steak, preferably cut about ½ inch (1.3 cm) thick
Kosher salt or coarse sea salt

DIP
1 cup (225 g) mayonnaise
1 pickled jalapeño, minced
2 tablespoons (20 g) minced onion
2 tablespoons (8 g) minced parsley
½ teaspoon soy sauce
¼ teaspoon ground white pepper
Lavash, other crackers, or zucchini rounds, for serving

1 Prepare the smoker for barbecuing, bringing the temperature to 200°F to 225°F (93°C to 107°C). If you are smoking at a slightly higher temperature, subtract a few minutes from the cooking time.

2 Sprinkle the tuna evenly with salt on both sides. Place it in the smoker directly on the grate, as far from the heat as possible. Cook the tuna for about 45 minutes. When it's done, it will be firm and no longer pink.

3 Cool the tuna briefly, and then chop it finely with a chef's knife rather than a food processor. You want a bit of texture. Transfer to a bowl and stir in the mayonnaise, jalapeño, onion, parsley, soy sauce, and white pepper. Refrigerate for at least 1 hour for the flavors to mingle. Let it sit at room temperature about 15 minutes before serving with lavash or other crackers.

Once you've tried smoked tuna, give smoked catfish a try. Catfish fillets smoke up so fast that you can have this spread out for snacking long before whatever you're really smoking is ready for the table.

SMOKED CATFISH SPREAD

PREPARATION TIME: 15 MINUTES, PLUS 30 MINUTES REFRIGERATION

COOKING TIME: ABOUT 45 MINUTES

MAKES ABOUT 2 CUPS (475 ML)

1 (8-ounce [225-g]) catfish fillet

1½ teaspoons coarsely ground black pepper

¾ teaspoon kosher salt or coarse sea salt

DIP

4 ounces (115 g) cream cheese

3 tablespoons (45 g) sour cream

1 tablespoon (10 g) minced onion

1 teaspoon dried dill weed

½ teaspoon freshly squeezed lemon juice

Kosher salt or coarse sea salt, optional

Crackers, small toasts, or cucumber rounds, for serving

1 Prepare the smoker for barbecuing, bringing the temperature to 200°F to 225°F (93°C to 107°C). If you are smoking at a slightly higher temperature, subtract a few minutes from the cooking time.

2 Sprinkle the catfish evenly with the black pepper and salt on both sides. Place the catfish in a small grill rack or piece of heavy-duty aluminum foil molded into a tray. Cook the catfish for about 45 minutes. When done, the catfish will be firm, opaque, and flaky.

3 Cool the catfish briefly and then flake the fish, discarding the skin and bones.

4 In a food processor, combine the fish with the cream cheese, sour cream, onion, dill, lemon juice, and kosher salt. Pulse a few times until well combined. Scrape the spread into a small serving bowl and refrigerate, covered, for at least 30 minutes for the flavors to mingle.

5 Let sit at room temperature about 15 minutes before serving with crackers, toasts, or cucumber rounds.

Adjust the ingredients as you wish, perhaps adding some diced avocado or fresh tiny tomatoes or subtracting the olives.

COCTEL DE CAMARÓN

PREPARATION TIME: 30 MINUTES, PLUS 30 MINUTES REFRIGERATION

COOKING TIME: ABOUT 20 MINUTES

SERVES 4

1 pound (455 g) peeled large shrimp (24 to 30)
1 tablespoon (15 ml) extra-virgin olive oil

COCTEL

1 (5.5-ounce [160-ml]) can Clamato or V-8 juice, chilled
1 tablespoon (15 ml) extra-virgin olive oil
Juice of 1 medium lime
½ cup (70 g) diced cucumber
½ cup (80 g) diced red onion
¼ cup (25 g) halved pimento-stuffed green olives
1 or 2 fresh serrano or jalapeño peppers, minced
Lime wedges, for garnish

1 Prepare the smoker for barbecuing, bringing the temperature to 200°F to 225°F (93°C to 107°C).

2 Toss the shrimp with the olive oil in a large bowl. Arrange them in a single layer on a small-mesh grill rack or a smokeproof dish large enough to hold them in a single layer.

3 Transfer the shrimp to the smoker, placing them as far from the heat as possible. The shrimp will be done in 15 to 20 minutes or when they are opaque, slightly firm, and lightly pink on the exterior. Let cool briefly and then chill for at least 30 minutes.

4 In another large bowl, gently stir the shrimp together with the Clamato, 1 tablespoon (15 ml) olive oil, lime juice, cucumber, onion, olives, and serrano. Spoon into margarita glasses or small bowls and serve.

If you love Vietnamese food, you can't do better than eating your way through twenty-first-century Houston. Start on Bellaire Boulevard and branch out from there. I like the Vietnamese technique of briefly soaking shrimp in a sugar and salt solution to add some tasty browned edges to them during their brief cooking. While typically grilled, shrimp take to the smoker like, well, shrimp to saltwater. Serve with butter lettuce leaves to wrap around a shrimp or two. I like to add some grated carrot or basil leaves or cilantro sprigs.

VIETNAMESE SHRIMP

PREPARATION TIME: ABOUT
15 MINUTES, PLUS 15 MINUTES
FOR MARINATING

COOKING TIME: ABOUT 20 MINUTES

SERVES 4 TO 6

½ cup (100 g) sugar

2 tablespoons (38 g) kosher salt
  or coarse sea salt

½ cup (120 ml) hot water

1 pound (455 g) peeled large shrimp
  (24 to 30)

2 tablespoons (28 ml) vegetable oil

4 cloves garlic, minced

2 teaspoons freshly ground
  black pepper

Butter lettuce leaves, shredded
  carrots, and basil leaves or cilantro
  sprigs, optional for serving

1   Prepare the smoker for barbecuing, bringing the temperature to 200°F to 225°F (93°C to 107°C).

2   Combine the sugar and salt in a bowl and mix with the hot water until mostly dissolved. Add the shrimp and give the mixture a good couple of stirs. Let sit for about 15 minutes. Drain and mix the shrimp with the oil, garlic, and black pepper.

3   Arrange the shrimp in a single layer on a small-mesh grill rack or a smoke-proof dish large enough to hold them in a single layer.

4   Transfer the shrimp to the smoker, placing them as far from the heat as possible. The shrimp will be done in 15 to 20 minutes or when opaque, slightly firm, and lightly pink on the exterior.

5   Serve the shrimp warm, wrapping them in lettuce and adding the other condiments as desired.

A photo of some luscious-looking smoked chicken wings tossed in an Alabama white barbecue sauce, which is based on mayonnaise, made me think of this approach. Any leftover dressing can top a wedge of iceberg lettuce or a baked potato.

SMOKED JALAPEÑO WINGS WITH HOT RANCH

PREPARATION TIME: 30 MINUTES, PLUS 30 MINUTES' REFRIGERATION

COOKING TIME: ABOUT 1½ HOURS

MAKES 3 DOZEN WINGS

18 chicken wings, halved at the joint
1 cup (235 ml) pickling liquid from
    a jar of pickled jalapeños
1 teaspoon kosher salt or coarse
    sea salt

HOT RANCH DRESSING
½ cup (120 ml) buttermilk
½ cup (115 g) mayonnaise
1 or 2 pickled jalapeños, sliced thin
½ teaspoon onion powder
½ teaspoon granulated garlic
½ teaspoon coarsely ground
    black pepper
¼ teaspoon kosher salt or coarse
    sea salt, plus more to taste

1 Combine the wings with the jalapeño liquid and salt in a gallon-size (3.8 L) zip-top bag and turn it a few times to coat the wings evenly. Refrigerate for about 1 hour.

2 Prepare the Hot Ranch Dressing, whisking together the buttermilk, mayonnaise, jalapeño, onion powder, granulated garlic, black pepper, and salt in a bowl. Taste and add additional salt if desired. Refrigerate until needed.

3 Prepare the smoker for barbecuing, bringing the temperature to 225°F to 250°F (107°C to 120°C). Oil a smokeproof baking pan or dish large enough to hold the wings in single layer.

4 Drain the wings and place them in the baking dish. Transfer the dish to the smoker.

5 After 1 hour of smoking, stir the wings well and brush them with about ½ cup (120 ml) dressing. Return the wings to the smoker for 15 to 30 minutes, until the chicken is cooked through and tender and the dressing is clinging to the wings. Serve hot with additional dressing for dunking and lots of napkins.

VARIATION: Korean Sesame Wings. *Skip the marinade and dressing. Instead, marinate the chicken wings in ¾ cup (175 ml) Korean soy sauce (ganjang) or Japanese soy sauce, along with 3 tablespoons (45 g) packed brown sugar, 2 tablespoons (28 ml) toasted sesame oil, 3 to 4 minced garlic cloves, and 1 tablespoon (22 g) Korean red pepper paste (gochujang) or sriracha. Marinate for at least 2 hours and up to overnight. Drain off and discard the marinade and cook following the instructions above. Top with sesame seeds and thin rounds of green onions to serve.*

Some folks put deviled eggs right into the smoker to add some wood character. I prefer this approach, where they get a lift from brisket.

BRISKET DEVILED EGGS

PREPARATION TIME: 45 MINUTES

MAKES 2 DOZEN DEVILED EGGS

1 dozen hard-boiled eggs, freshly
   prepared
¼ cup plus 2 tablespoons (88 g)
   mayonnaise
1 tablespoon (15 g) Dijon mustard
½ teaspoon prepared horseradish
Kosher salt or coarse sea salt
Freshly ground black pepper
1 cup (225 g) shredded barbecued
   brisket, warm
Fresh chives, fresh jalapeño or
   serrano pepper rounds, or tiny
   squares of red bell pepper,
   optional for serving

1   While they're still warm, peel the hard-boiled eggs. Scoop the yolks out of the eggs into a bowl and then mash them with a fork or grate them on the small holes of a box grater. Mix the yolks with the mayonnaise, mustard, horseradish, and salt and black pepper to taste. Spoon the mixture back into eggs, keeping it rather flat.

2   Top each egg half with finely shredded warm barbecued brisket, about a teaspoon or two per half. Top with a few bits of chives, a round of jalapeño or serrano, or a bit of red bell pepper, if you wish. Chill before serving, if desired.

I've never been a fan of most smoked nuts available commercially, which are usually soaked in liquid smoke. I always think they belong at some cocktail party from the 1950s. Whether your style is retro or of the moment, these pecans, enhanced with real smoke, will be a welcome treat. Smoke them over pecan wood if you have it.

SMOKE-SCENTED PECANS

PREPARATION TIME: 15 MINUTES

COOKING TIME: ABOUT 30 MINUTES

MAKES ABOUT 2 CUPS (475 ML)

1 tablespoon (14 g) salted butter
   or bacon drippings
1 tablespoon (15 g) packed light
   or dark brown sugar
¼ teaspoon garlic powder
¼ teaspoon ground cayenne
Kosher salt or coarse sea salt
8 ounces (225 g, about 2 cups)
   unsalted pecan halves

1   Prepare your smoker for barbecuing, bringing the temperature to 225°F to 250°F (107°C to 120°C).

2   In a medium skillet, melt the butter with the sugar, garlic powder, and cayenne. Stir in the pecans and coat well. Stir in the salt, adding only enough to give the nuts a mild saltiness. Transfer the nuts to a shallow, smokeproof dish or a piece of heavy-duty foil molded into a small tray.

3   Place the tray of pecans in the smoker and cook until dried and fragrant, 25 to 30 minutes.

4   Transfer the pecans to absorbent paper to cool. Serve right away or keep in a covered jar for several days.

I used to turn my nose up at the ubiquitous "cocktail" sausage, but I've come to admire how darned cute they are. Like so many foods, adding a fresh whiff of wood smoke to the already lightly smoked little wieners or "piglets" just improves on them. The accompanying Jezebel sauce, a condiment loved throughout the South, is a natural for Texas with its sweet heat.

PIGLETS IN JEZEBEL SAUCE

PREPARATION TIME: 15 MINUTES

COOKING TIME: ABOUT 45 MINUTES

SERVES 8 OR MORE AS A NIBBLE

JEZEBEL SAUCE

¾ cup (240 g) apple jelly

¾ cup (240 g) pineapple or apricot preserves

¼ cup (60 g) whole-grain or brown mustard

2 tablespoons (30 g) prepared horseradish

½ teaspoon red pepper flakes

2 pounds (900 g) cocktail sausages, such as Lit'l Smokies

1   Make the Jezebel Sauce, combining the apple jelly, preserves, mustard, horseradish, and red pepper flakes in a medium bowl. Whisk until smooth.

2   Prepare your smoker for barbecuing, bringing the temperature to 225°F to 250°F (107°C to 120°C).

3   Arrange the cocktail sausages in a large cast-iron skillet or smokeproof shallow baking dish. Transfer to the smoker and cook for 30 to 45 minutes until plump and heated through. Pour the sauce over the sausages, stir together, and return to the smoker for about 15 minutes more until the sauce is warm.

4   Serve from the skillet or dish with bamboo skewers or fondue forks for spearing the sausages.

One of the simplest snacks to sustain a barbecuer during a long cook is the humble hot dog. It's nearly always possible to poke a few dogs into the nooks and crannies on the cooking grate, regardless of your main smoking project. They're fairly forgiving about the temperature at which you're cooking too. I mention of couple of especially good nationally available hot dogs, but many Texas butcher shops and even supermarkets make their own. If you want, skip the mentioned mustard and relish for one of the barbecue sauces included in this book.

HOT DOG!

PREPARATION TIME: LESS THAN
5 MINUTES

COOKING TIME: ABOUT 45 MINUTES

SERVES AS MANY AS YOU WISH

Good quality all-beef hot dogs, such
   as Hebrew National or Vienna Beef
Squishy white bread hot dogs buns
   or warm thick flour tortillas
Mustard
Pickle relish or chopped pickled
   jalapeño peppers, or a combination
Chopped onions

1   Prepare the smoker for barbecuing, bringing the temperature to 200°F to 275°F (93°C to 140°C).

2   Transfer the hot dogs to the smoker and cook until the skins look ready to burst, about 45 minutes to 1 hour.

3   Serve right away on buns or tortillas, with all the trimmings.

CHAPTER 5

BEEF: THE SACRED COW OF TEXAS Q

Some Southern pitmasters might say Texans started barbecuing beef simply because they couldn't tell a steer from a pig. The pork and beef barbecue traditions are entirely different animals in all respects, including origins. British colonists brought pigs to the East Coast and adopted Native American cooking methods to create their style of barbecue, which was perfected by African-American pitmasters. Long before these settlers moved west, Mexican ranchers and *vaqueros*, the earliest cowboys, introduced the Southwest to their specialty, *barbacoa de cabeza*. It's whole head barbecue, preferably made with a big steer's head that is smoked overnight in an underground pit. German butchers in Central Texas intervened around the turn of the century to change the nature of beef barbecue. For them, sweetbreads, brains, and other parts of the head were too much of a delicacy to put in a pit. They took up barbecuing as a way to get rid of their worst cuts of beef, like brisket. The thrifty butchers found that long, slow smoking tenderized even the toughest meat, turning an unwanted cut into a magical dish, not to mention a profitable sideline. The glorification of brisket today and its position at the top of any menu make it hard to imagine a time when it lacked prestige. However, it's not alone in commercial or backyard barbecue pits today.

"Many Texas barbecue fanatics have a strong belief in the beneficial properties of accumulated grease."

—CALVIN TRILLIN,
TRILLIN ON TEXAS

As venerable as brisket is in Texas barbecue, it's a relatively recent phenomenon. Up until the 1970s, whole carcasses were commonly shipped, necessitating the use of, well, the whole critter. From the 1970s forward, butchers and supermarkets could order specific pieces of meat, and brisket began its ascendency. However you choose to barbecue a full brisket (called "packer trim" or "packer cut"), it takes some attention, skill, and preferably a "stick burner," a pit that burns logs for its heat source as well for the aroma of smoke. This cut keeps the fat cap completely intact on the brisket, and it doesn't mess with wrapping the meat, sometimes referred to as the "Texas crutch." You add smoke from beginning to end, and the flavor intensifies as the brisket shrinks significantly during its cooking time, even with the use of a beer-infused mop to help keep the meat moist and add another nuance of flavor. In our family, this is always cooked over oak.

CLASSIC CENTRAL TEXAS BRISKET

PREPARATION TIME: 1 HOUR, PLUS
OVERNIGHT MARINATING

COOKING TIME: 10 TO 14 HOURS

SERVES 12 OR MORE

2 cups (280 g) Wild Willy's Number
    One-derful Rub (see page 43)
1 (10- to 12-pound [4.5- to 5.4-kg])
    packer-trimmed beef brisket

BASIC BEER MOP
12 ounces (355 ml) beer, preferably
    medium bodied
½ cup (120 ml) cider vinegar
½ cup (120 ml) water
¼ cup (60 ml) vegetable oil
½ medium onion, chopped
2 cloves garlic, minced
1 tablespoon (15 ml)
    Worcestershire sauce

1 To marinate overnight, combine the rub ingredients in a small bowl. Set aside 1 tablespoon (10 g) of the rub to add to the mop. Apply the rub evenly to the brisket, massaging it in well. Get the rub into every pore of the meat. Place the brisket in a plastic bag and refrigerate.

2 The next day remove the brisket from the refrigerator and discard the plastic bag. Let the brisket sit at room temperature for 45 minutes.

3 Prepare the smoker for barbecuing, bringing the temperature to 200°F to 220°F (93°C to 104°C).

4 In a saucepan, mix together the beer, vinegar, water, oil, onion, garlic, Worcestershire sauce, and rub and warm over low heat.

5 Transfer the brisket to the coolest part of the smoker, placing it directly on the grate, fat-side up, so the juices will help baste the meat. Cook the brisket until well done and tender, 1 to 1¼ hours per pound (455 g). Every hour or so, baste the blackening hunk with the mop.

6 When the brisket is well done with a good crusty bark and an internal temperature of just over 200°F (93°C), remove it from the smoker and let it sit at room temperature for 30 to 45 minutes. If you wish, cut the fatty top section away from the leaner bottom portion. An easily identifiable layer of fat separates the two areas. Trim the excess fat from both pieces and slice them thinly against the grain. Watch carefully as you slice because the grain changes direction. Some folks will want the leaner brisket, others the moister or fattier. You'll have plenty of both.

VARIATION: West Texas Mesquite-Smoked "Cowboy" Brisket. *You need mesquite logs or large chunks for this and a burn barrel (page 36). Burn wood down to glowing coals and add it to the smoker as needed to keep the fire going. Cook at about 300°F (150°C) for around 50 minutes per pound (455 g).*

This method of brisket preparation owes a lot to Aaron Franklin as well as to the fine folks behind Camp Brisket at Texas A&M University, sponsored by Texas Foodways. You'll want a brisket graded Prime for this version. Central Texas barbecue is typically cooked over oak. If you want some sauce, try out Thin and Tangy Barbecue Sauce (page 145), but use it judiciously.

SALT-AND-PEPPER CENTRAL TEXAS BRISKET

PREPARATION TIME: 1 HOUR, PLUS OVERNIGHT MARINATING

COOKING TIME: 10 TO 14 HOURS

SERVES 12 OR MORE

¾ cup (125 g) Dalmatian Rub (page 43)

1 (10- to 12-pound [4.5- to 5.4-kg]) USDA Prime packer-trimmed beef brisket, fat cap trimmed to ¼ inch (6 mm) thick

½ cup (120 ml) Worcestershire sauce

½ cup (120 ml) cider or white vinegar

1   The night before you plan to barbecue, combine the Dalmation Rub in a small bowl. Apply the rub evenly to the brisket, massaging it in well. Get the rub into every pore of the meat. Place the brisket in a plastic bag and refrigerate it overnight.

2   The next day, when you're ready to barbecue, prepare the smoker for barbecuing, bringing the temperature to 250°F to 275°F (120°C to 140°C).

3   Before you begin to barbecue, remove the brisket from the refrigerator and discard the plastic bag. Let the brisket sit at room temperature for 45 minutes.

4   Combine the Worcestershire sauce and vinegar in a spray bottle for spritzing the meat.

5   Transfer the brisket to the coolest part of the smoker, placing it directly on the grate, fat-side up, so the juices will help baste the meat. Cook the brisket until well done and tender, about 1 to 1¼ hours per pound (455 g). Every hour or so, spray the blackening hunk with the Worcestershire-vinegar mixture. After 6 hours, spritz the brisket again and wrap it in unwaxed butcher paper. Return the wrapped brisket to the smoker and continue cooking until the meat reaches an internal temperature of 200°F (93°C). Rather than poking holes in the paper to take your beef's temperature, try to get a sense of its doneness by feel, as it gets more flexible and supple in its final hour or so of cooking.

6   When the brisket is ready, remove it from the smoker and let it sit at room temperature, still wrapped, about 1 hour until the meat's internal temperature has dropped to 145°F to 150°F (63°C to 66°C). (If you don't plan to serve it after 1 hour, place the wrapped brisket in a cooler to keep warm for at least 1 more hour.) If you wish, cut the fatty top section away from the leaner bottom portion. An easily identifiable layer of fat separates the two areas. Slice the brisket thinly against the grain. Watch carefully as you slice because the grain changes direction. Some folks will want the leaner brisket, others the moister or fattier. You'll have plenty of both.

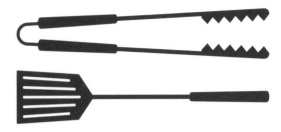

Camp Brisket

A fantasy camp in College Station for aspiring and accomplished barbecuers, Camp Brisket combines food, fire, and science. My fellow participants in camp included defense attorneys, IT guys, pitmasters, petroleum geologists, and even a former Texas resident with a restaurant in Bali. I was something of an anomaly because the group skewed decidedly male, but I was as warmly welcomed as those guys. It's a program of Foodways Texas with Texas A&M University's Meat Science Section of the Department of Animal Science. You'll learn all about the anatomy of a cow and check out differences in meat of different grades cooked over different wood on different styles of equipment. While eating great Q, you'll rub shoulders and chat with an all-star roster of pitmasters, meat scientists, and equipment manufacturers. You'll pay for the privilege, but it's worth every cent. You can bet I bought a Camp Brisket T-shirt and wear it proudly. The only challenge is getting in the early January annual event. The camp is so popular that you have to register for a lottery at foodwaystexas.org. If that's not enough education for you, the two groups also offer a Barbecue Summer Camp, which covers our favorite subject more broadly.

Little crispy critters of meat goodness, burnt ends are perhaps the highest calling of the fattier "point" portion of a brisket. You have a couple of ways of going about achieving burnt ends. Know that you'll need a few hours of cooking time beyond the average brisket, whichever technique you go with. You can start with the point already barbecued. Slice it away from the leaner "flat" cut and put it back on the smoker right away in a pan with a saucy combo of ingredients. If you're ready to eat and would rather make the burnt ends the following day, wrap the point in butcher paper, cool, and refrigerate. Then, fire up your smoker the next day to finish the burnt ends. The other method has you starting the cook with just a raw brisket point cut. Check a good-size supermarket with a real meat counter or talk to the proprietor of a meat market or butcher shop. In Texas, check HEB, Central Market, Market Street, or smaller local shops for the cut.

GLAZED BRISKET BURNT ENDS

PREPARATION TIME: ABOUT 1 HOUR

COOKING TIME: 2 TO 2½ HOURS IF STARTING FROM A SMOKED BRISKET, OR 8 TO 8 ½ HOURS IF STARTING FROM SCRATCH

SERVES 4 TO 6

STARTING FROM A SMOKED BRISKET

1 fully barbecued fatty top section of Classic Central Texas Brisket (page 67) or other barbecued brisket

12 ounces (355 ml) Dr Pepper, TexaCola (from Southside Craft Soda in San Antonio), or other cola

½ cup (120 g) barbecue sauce, such as Sweet Onion and Black Pepper Sauce (page 143)

2 tablespoons (30 g) packed light or dark brown sugar

2 tablespoons (20 g) dry rub used initially on the brisket

2 tablespoons (28 g) salted butter

1   Prepare the smoker for barbecuing, bringing the temperature to 225°F to 250°F (107°C to 120°C).

2   Slice the cooked brisket into approximately 1-inch (2.5-cm) cubes. Trim away any large hunks of surface fat. Arrange the brisket cubes in a shallow foil pan or large smokeproof baking dish.

3   In a medium saucepan, bring the Dr Pepper, barbecue sauce, brown sugar, dry rub, and butter to a quick boil over high heat. Pour the glaze mixture evenly over the brisket cubes. Transfer the brisket pan back to the smoker. Continue smoking for another 2 to 2½ hours, stirring the burnt ends once after about 1½ hours. The burnt ends are ready when the liquid has evaporated or been absorbed by the meat, which should be dark, crusty, and somewhat caramelized. Serve right away.

STARTING FROM SCRATCH

¼ cup (42 g) Dalmatian Rub (page
  43) or another favorite dry rub
1 uncooked brisket point cut, about
  5 pounds (2.3 kg)
½ cup (120 ml) Vinegar Spritz
  (page 49)
12 ounces (355 ml) Dr Pepper,
  TexaCola (from Southside Craft
  Soda in San Antonio), or other cola
½ cup (120 g) tomato-based
  barbecue sauce, such as Sweet
  Onion and Black Pepper Sauce
  (page 143)
2 tablespoons (30 g) packed light
  or dark brown sugar
2 tablespoons (28 g) salted butter

1 Prepare the smoker for barbecuing, bringing the temperature to 225°F to
    250°F (107°C to 120°C).

2 Set aside 1 tablespoon (10 g) of the Dalmatian Rub to add to the glaze.
    Massage the rest of the dry rub into the brisket, getting into the cracks
    and crevices.

3 Combine the vinegar and Worcestershire sauce in a spray bottle.

4 Transfer the brisket to the smoker, placing it directly on the grate, and cook
    until well done and tender, about 200°F (93°C), approximately 1 to 1¼ hours
    per pound (455 kg). Every hour or so, or when you need to add wood or open
    the smoker for any other reason, spray the blackening hunk lightly with the
    spritz.

5 When the brisket is done, remove it from the smoker (you will return it to the
    smoker shortly). Slice the brisket into approximately 1-inch (2.5 cm) cubes.
    Trim away any large hunks of surface fat. Arrange the brisket cubes in a
    shallow foil pan or large smokeproof baking dish.

6 In a medium saucepan, bring the Dr Pepper, barbecue sauce, brown sugar,
    dry rub, and butter to a quick boil over high heat. Pour the glaze mixture
    evenly over the brisket cubes. Transfer the pan back to the smoker. Continue
    smoking for another 2 to 2½ hours, stirring the burnt ends once after about
    1½ hours. The burnt ends are ready when the liquid has evaporated or been
    absorbed by the meat, which should be dark, crusty, and somewhat caramel-
    ized. Serve right away.

This might be my very favorite way to eat brisket—at least today. In Spanish, salpicón *refers to a hash or toss up of sorts. Mind you, a classic salpicón of the far southwest corner of Texas, where it meets old and New Mexico, is traditionally made with long-simmered brisket. I started using a smoked version of the meat. By the way, I give you permission to use brisket barbecued by a local pitmaster too. It's sure a timesaver if you have a good option in your neighborhood. Break out the margaritas.*

EL PASO SALPICÓN

PREPARATION TIME: 1 HOUR

SERVES 10 TO 12

DRESSING

¾ cup (175 ml) extra-virgin olive oil

¼ cup (60 g) chipotle mayonnaise, such as Real Foods

½ cup (120 ml) freshly squeezed lime juice

½ teaspoon kosher salt or coarse sea salt, plus more to taste

SALAD

3 pounds (1.4 kg) shredded barbecued beef brisket, such as Classic Central Texas Brisket (page 67), warm

3 red-ripe plum tomatoes, diced

1 medium red or yellow bell pepper, diced

6 ounces (170 g) asadero or Monterey Jack cheese, diced

6 medium radishes, sliced very thin

½ cup (80 g) diced red onion

1 fresh jalapeño pepper, minced

Inner leaves of 1 head romaine, sliced into thin ribbons

1 large avocado, diced

½ cup (70 g) pepitas (hulled pumpkin seeds)

½ cup (8 g) chopped fresh cilantro

1   Whisk the olive oil, mayonnaise, lime juice, and ½ teaspoon salt together in a medium bowl. Taste and add more salt, if you wish.

2   In a large bowl, combine half of the dressing with the brisket and let sit for 15 to 30 minutes.

3   Before serving, add to the brisket the tomatoes, bell pepper, cheese, radishes, onion, and jalapeño. Arrange the romaine on a serving platter. Spoon the brisket mixture over the romaine and then scatter with the avocado, pepitas, and cilantro. Drizzle more dressing over the *salpicón* as desired.

Few morning foods have a stronger fan club than breakfast tacos, especially around Austin and San Antonio. In fact, these days, breakfast tacos are just about as a big a deal as barbecue itself. To the uninitiated, they may look a little overhyped. Simple in concept and execution, breakfast tacos consist of a soft flour tortilla folded over a filling of meat, perhaps chorizo, bacon, or even German sausage, with maybe eggs, beans, or potatoes. Often leftovers from dinner the night before fill the tortillas. Traditionally they have little embellishment beyond a table salsa. Well-made, these icons serve as one of the finest ways to kick off any day. What could be better than stuffing the breakfast taco with barbecued brisket, for a double Texas treasure? If you haven't barbecued your own meat, it's worth picking some up from a favorite joint, just to whip the tacos up. I prefer these with the brisket shredded and mixed into a scramble but you could simply slice warm brisket and snuggle some scrambled eggs beside it in a warm tortilla. I like the extra step of brushing the tacos with butter and crisping them just a touch under the broiler but you can skip that step if you want to chow down five minutes sooner.

BRISKET-AND-EGG BREAKFAST TACOS

PREPARATION TIME: 30 MINUTES

COOKING TIME: 15 MINUTES

SERVES 4

12 ounces (340 g) shredded
  barbecued brisket
1 tablespoon (14 g) unsalted butter
  (optional)
4 large eggs, lightly whisked with
  1 tablespoon (15 ml) water
Kosher salt or coarse sea salt
  (optional)
12 flour tortillas, preferably
  medium-thick and about 6 inches
  (15 cm) in diameter, warmed
8 ounces (225 g) shredded mild
  Cheddar, Monterey Jack or Pepper
  Jack cheese
Several tablespoons melted unsalted
  butter
Pico de gallo or other favorite salsa
  or hot sauce

1   Preheat the broiler. Grease a baking sheet.

2   In a medium skillet, warm the brisket over medium heat. If it doesn't give off enough fat to coat the bottom of the skillet, add the optional butter and let it melt and give the mixture a good stir. Pour in the egg mixture and reduce the heat to low. You may want to add salt, depending on the seasoning of the brisket itself. Stir the eggs into the brisket and continue stirring until soft moist curds form around the meat a matter of only a few minutes. Remove from the heat before the eggs get dry looking. Give another couple of stirs and then spoon the mixture equally into the tortillas, sprinkle each with a portion of cheese, place on the baking sheet, and then fold each over as you go.

3   Brush the tacos with the melted butter and pop under the broiler for 2 minutes or until lightly crisp on top. Serve right away, accompanied by salsa.

A DOZEN OTHER BARBECUED BRISKET RIFFS

Brisket Grilled Cheese. For a pair of sandwiches, grate 8 ounces (225 g) Cheddar or other mild melting cheese. Generously butter one side each of four good-size slices of farmhouse-style bread. Warm a griddle or large cast-iron skillet over medium heat. Arrange the bread slices on the griddle, buttered-sides down. Scatter the cheese evenly over all four slices. When the cheese has begun to melt, arrange about ⅓ cup (75 g) warm barbecued brisket over two of the bread slices. When the bread is toasted brown on the bottom side and the cheese has melted, place the two bread slices with just cheese over the brisket-topped bread. Serve right away with some tangy pickles on the side or in the sandwich.

Brisket Bowl o' Red. Well, you probably want to serve at least a couple of bowls o' red. Make a Tex-Mex-style chili gravy: Pour 2 teaspoons oil into a large saucepan and then heat and add about ¾ cup (120 g) chopped onion and 1 or 2 minced garlic cloves and cook until the onion's translucent. Stir in ¼ cup (30 g) Texas-style chili powder, such as Gebhardt's, and, if you wish, some ground cumin. Pour in 2 cups (475 ml) water and simmer together for about 15 minutes over medium heat. Mix in 2 cups (450 g) barbecued brisket that has been pulled into small bite-size shreds and simmer for another 15 minutes. Add salt and, if you would like more heat, a few shakes ground cayenne. The liquid should be thick and not too soupy. Cook a bit longer if needed. Serve in bowls with some chopped onion.

Brisket Bánh Mì. For a twist on the classic Vietnamese sandwich, use an 8-inch (20 cm) section of soft baguette for each sandwich. Slice horizontally, leaving a "hinge" at the back of the baguette, and cover both sides with mayonnaise. I add a squiggle of sriracha too. Mix 4 ounces (115 g) warm barbecued brisket with a teaspoon or two each of fish sauce and rice vinegar. Add the brisket to the sandwich and then stuff with thin-sliced radishes, carrots, and cucumbers. Garnish with fresh cilantro and enjoy.

Brisket Pho. Use any good-sounding Vietnamese beef pho recipe but, in making the broth, replace about one-third of the meat called for with barbecued beef brisket. Add slices of brisket to the soup along with other garnishes as you wish.

Smoke-Stickers. Plump up potstickers, the soft but chewy Chinese dumplings, with barbecued brisket as the meat for the filling. For about two dozen potstickers, combine 1½ cups (338 g) shredded brisket in a food processor with ¾ cup (23 g) chopped fresh spinach or chard, 2 green onions, 2 teaspoons minced fresh ginger, 1 egg white, 1 tablespoon (15 ml) soy sauce, and 1 garlic clove. Process until fairly finely chopped but short of pureed. Place a heaping teaspoon of filling on a round or square wonton wrapper. Moisten the edge with a bit of water and seal in a half-moon or triangle. Repeat with wonton wrappers until you have used all of the filling. Make a sauce of ½ teaspoon cornstarch with ⅔ cup (160 ml) chicken stock, 2 tablespoons (38 g) Chinese plum sauce or plum jelly, and 1 teaspoon soy sauce. In a 12-inch (30 cm) skillet, warm a splash of oil over high heat. Fry the potstickers for 2 minutes or until the bottoms of the dumplings are deep golden brown. Give the sauce a stir and pour it quickly over the dumplings. Immediately cover the skillet and reduce the heat to medium-low. Steam the dumplings for 2 minutes. Uncover and raise the heat again to high. Cook just a minute or two until the sauce has reduced to a thick glaze. Serve immediately.

Frito Pie. This is a true Texas favorite with a San Antonio birthplace. For everyone you plan to serve, first layer a big handful of Fritos (no, nothing else will do here) in a shallow bowl or plate. Spoon over about 1 cup (235 ml) of your favorite chili. Scatter ½ cup to 1 cup (113 to 225 g) warm barbecued brisket shreds over the chili and then top with handfuls of grated mild Cheddar and chopped iceberg or romaine lettuce. Garnish with chopped tomatoes and chopped onions. Serve right away.

Crispy Brisket Tacos with Hot Ranch. Stir about 1 tablespoon (9 g) minced pickled jalapeño and a few grinds black pepper into 1 cup (235 ml) ranch dressing.

To make a dozen crisp tacos, first heat about ½ inch (1.3 cm) of vegetable oil in a heavy skillet over medium-high heat. Have several layers of paper towels nearby and also a baking rack arranged over some additional paper towels. Dunk each tortilla quickly in the hot oil, just long enough for it to turn limp, a few seconds for each. Lay the softened tortillas on the paper towels. Spoon about 2 tablespoons (28 g) shredded smoked brisket across the center of each tortilla. Fold up and secure the top with a toothpick. Return a couple of tacos to the hot oil and fry first on one side and then the other, about 30 seconds per side, just until crisp. Drain well over the skillet and then set on the baking rack. Fry the remaining tacos. Remove the toothpicks, add the ranch dressing, and eat while piping hot.

Soft Brisket Tacos with Barbecue Vinaigrette.
Make a slaw topping by stirring together 2 tablespoons (28 ml) vegetable oil with 1 tablespoon (15 ml) white vinegar, ½ teaspoon freshly ground black pepper, and a heaping ¼ teaspoon salt in a medium bowl. Add about ½ teaspoon crushed dried red chile, if you wish, and then mix in 1½ cups (105 g) shredded green cabbage and 1 tablespoon (10 g) minced onion. Refrigerate briefly while preparing the sauce and the tacos. Make the vinaigrette by stirring together 1 tablespoon (15 g) smoky barbecue sauce, 1 tablespoon (15 ml) cider or white vinegar, and ¼ cup (60 ml) vegetable oil in a small bowl. Season to taste with salt and pepper and a bit more oil if you wish. Warm a dozen corn tortillas in a steamer or wrapped in foil in a 300°F (150°C, or gas mark 2) oven for 15 minutes or so. Layer two tortillas together, one on top of the other, to make six sturdier tacos. Spoon about 3 tablespoons (42 g) warm shredded barbecued brisket or burnt ends down the center of each tortilla pair. With a slotted spoon, add a tablespoon or two of the slaw to each taco and then drizzle with a scant tablespoon of vinaigrette. Eat right away.

Brisket Nachos.
Pick out a quantity of good-size unbroken chips from a bag of tortilla chips. Top each individually with a smear of warm refried beans across each chip before building upwards. Toppings should include grated melting cheeses such as mild Cheddar or Monterey Jack, sliced fresh or pickled jalapeño slices, and shreds of barbecued brisket. Arrange the nachos neatly on a baking sheet and cook in a 375°F (190°C, or gas mark 5) oven until the cheese is melted, about 5 minutes. Transfer to a decorative platter and eat immediately, perhaps with salsa or guacamole on the side.

Brisket Breakfast Sandwiches.
Start with English muffins or homemade or good-quality store-bought biscuits, preferably about 3 inches (7.5 cm) across. If the biscuits are hot from the oven, simply split and butter them. If they're not quite so fresh, split, butter, and toast the insides of the biscuits on a griddle. Cover one half of each warm muffin or biscuit with a thin slice of melting cheese such as mild Cheddar, mozzarella, or pepper Jack. Fry the same number of eggs as you have biscuits. They work best on sandwiches fried just beyond over easy to over hard. Place a warm egg over the cheese and then top with about ½ cup (56 g) warm shredded barbecued brisket. If you have something tangy like chutney, it's a great addition. A little spoonful of barbecue sauce or barbecue sauce mixed with mayo can be drizzled on too. Add the top halves of the biscuits to make a sandwich and you're good to go.

Brisket Hash.
In a large heavy skillet, warm several tablespoons of oil over medium heat and stir in about 2 cups (220 g) diced potatoes, a large diced onion, and a diced red or green bell pepper. Cook until the potatoes have begun to soften, about 10 minutes. Stir in 4 cups (900 g) shredded barbecued brisket along with ½ cup (120 ml) beef stock and a tablespoon or two (14 to 30 g) of mustard and ketchup or barbecue sauce. Cover the skillet and cook for 10 minutes. Uncover the skillet and scrape the hash back up and down over several more minutes until the liquid is absorbed and the mixture gets some crusty edges on the bottom. Serve with poached eggs for an extra-special treat.

Bagels with a Brisket Schmear.
These are decidedly not kosher but tasty indeed. Combine ½ cup (113 g) chopped or shredded warm brisket with 8 ounces (225 g) cream cheese in a food processor until smooth. Spread the mixture on split plain or savory flavored bagels, toasted if you wish. Sprinkle with chives or finely sliced green onions and serve.

Brisket isn't at the center of every Texas barbecue plate, especially along the eastern side of the state and anywhere that the Q has been influenced by Southern African-American traditions. Here, the cut is beef clod or shoulder, or a chuck roast if the other's not available. The beef is often cooked at a higher temperature than brisket, and because of its smaller size, it should be ready in 4 or 5 hours rather than brisket's sunup-to-sundown or overnight cook. If you have hickory, this is a great time to use it. Serve the beef chopped with lots of molasses-y sauce, either on the plate or in buns.

SAUCY EAST TEXAS CHOPPED BEEF SANDWICHES

PREPARATION TIME: 30 MINUTES

COOKING TIME: ABOUT 5 HOURS

SERVES 8 TO 10

3 tablespoons (33 g) yellow mustard
½ cup (83 g) Dalmatian Rub
   (page 43)
2 teaspoons granulated garlic
1 (5- to 6-pound [2.3- to 2.7-kg]) beef
   shoulder roast or chuck roast
East Texas Molasses BBQ Sauce
   (page 141) or another sweet
   tomato-based barbecue sauce
Sturdy burger buns, optional

1 Combine the Dalmatian Rub with the granulated garlic in a small bowl. Rub the mustard over all surfaces of the beef. Cover the beef in the dry rub and massage it in well. Let the beef sit at room temperature.

2 Prepare the smoker for barbecuing, bringing the temperature to 300°F to 325°F (150°C to 170°C).

3 Transfer the beef to the smoker, placing it directly on the grate, and cook for about 5 hours. After 2 hours, wrap it in heavy-duty foil and return to the smoker for 2 more hours. Unwrap the beef, saving any drippings, and return it to the smoker for about 1 hour more until the meat is well done and an instant-read thermometer inserted deep into the roast reads 200°F (93°C). Chop the meat, discarding any fat, and mix the meat drippings back into it. Mix as much barbecue sauce as you like into the meat. Serve with buns to make sandwiches, if desired.

VARIATION: **Beef Shoulder, Lockhart Style.** *Serve sliced rather than chopped with only the meat juices. Offer onion slices on the side.*

Insane and Insanely Good Barbecue Sandwiches

Sure, you can make a grand sandwich with just sliced, chopped, or shredded beef—whether it be from the shoulder, brisket, or another cut—and some sauce. However, there's quite a wondrous world of other sandwiches being built by pitmasters across the state. CBQ in Schertz adds chives and blue cheese to its chopped and sauced brisket sandwich. Brisket with sliced smoked sausage piled high on a bun or bread is arguably the most common combo. You can find one of those everywhere from the New Zion Missionary Baptist Church in Huntsville to Austin's Franklin Barbecue. Slaw, dill pickles, onions, and sauce are all worthy additions. Pecan Lodge in Dallas adds pulled pork to brisket and sausage as well as slaw, sauce, and jalapeños. At Austin's LA Barbecue, get a LA Frito Loco with chopped beef, pulled pork, chipotle slaw, beans, cheese, jalapeños, and yes, Fritos, on a bun. Jambo's BBQ Shack in Rendon does a combo of chopped and sliced brisket with pulled pork, a bologna slice, a link sausage, and a couple of pork ribs just to make it truly impossible to eat out of hand, all constructed on Texas toast. Are you sitting down for this one? The Jailbreak, conceived by The Pit BBQ in San Angelo, combines sliced brisket with peanut butter and jelly on a toasted bun. I confess I haven't tried it. Not all sandwiches rely on beef for their substance. As just one example, a few years back, Daniel Vaughn at Texas Monthly named the Mother Clucker chicken sandwich at Stanley's Famous Pit BBQ in Tyler as his favorite sandwich in the state. On jalapeño sourdough, a smoked chicken thigh, fried egg, candied bacon, and Cheddar are piled high and drizzled with spicy barbecue mayo. Oh yeah, and you can add guacamole if you like.

Nearly as iconic as brisket these days is the big honking beef rib that looks like it might have come from a brontosaurus. In a couple of decades, these have gone from being as scarce among barbecuers as dinos themselves to one of the most popular beef dishes to smoke in the pit. Generous marbling and consistent thickness and grain make them a much simpler meat to perfect than a gnarly brisket, perhaps part of the reason for their popularity today. These ribs come from the "plate primal," and ideally you want the ribs from smack in the center of the ribcage, ribs 6, 7, and 8 in butcher speak. These come out crusty yet moist, and their magnitude just screams "BBQ master!" Talk to a butcher ahead to make sure the cut is available when you want it.

DINO SHORT RIBS

PREPARATION TIME: 30 MINUTES

COOKING TIME: ABOUT 6 HOURS

SERVES AT LEAST 6

¾ cup (125 g) Dalmatian Rub
  (page 43)
2 (3-bone) primal plate racks uncut
  beef ribs
1 batch Beer Mop for Beef and
  Just about Everything (page 47)

1 Massage the dry rub all over the rib racks and let them sit at room temperature for about 30 minutes.

2 Prepare the smoker for barbecuing, bringing the temperature to 225°F to 250°F (107°C to 120°C).

3 Heat the mop in a saucepan over low heat and keep it warm while you're cooking.

4 Transfer the ribs to the smoker, placing them directly on the grate, meaty side up. Cook for about 6 hours total until well done with meat that pulls away from the bones but is short of falling off the bones. During the first 3 hours, mop every 45 minutes to 1 hour in a wood-burning pit or as appropriate for your style of smoker. After 3 hours, remove the ribs from the smoker and lay each rack on a piece of heavy-duty aluminum foil twice the size of the rack. Splash a couple tablespoons of mop over each rib rack. Close up the two foil packages and return them to the smoker for 2 hours more. Unwrap the ribs, discarding the foil, and return the ribs to the smoker. The beef will recede from the bones somewhat as it smokes. Cook for an additional 45 minutes to 1 hour until crusted and well done.

5 Remove the ribs from the smoker and let them sit for about 15 minutes or until cool enough to handle. Slice between the ribs to separate them and serve.

VARIATION: **Korean-Sauced Short Ribs.** *After removing the ribs from the foil and before returning them to the smoker, brush the ribs thickly with Korean Barbecue Sauce (page 147).*

South Texas vaqueros initially popularized wood-fire cooked skirt steak served in or with tortillas. Barbecuing the meat just ups that savory range of flavor. If you add an onion and a bell pepper to the smoker, they'll be ready in about the same time as the meat. Here's one of the handful of times that I like a marinade for beef rather than a dry rub because skirt steak is so filled with nooks and crannies to flavor with the liquid. I like a final flourish of garlic butter on the meat before slicing it, but that's gilding the lily. Serve with Pintos with Pico (page 153) and Mexican Street Corn Salad (page 162).

CERVEZA-SOAKED FAJITAS

PREPARATION TIME: 45 MINUTES, PLUS 8 TO 12 HOURS FOR MARINATING

COOKING TIME: 1¼ HOURS

SERVES 6 TO 8

ORANGE MARINADE

1 cup (235 ml) orange juice

1 large onion, chopped or sliced into thin rings

4 tablespoons (56 g) salted butter, melted

3 tablespoons (45 ml) Worcestershire sauce

2 tablespoons (18 g) dry mustard

2 tablespoons (20 g) Red Dirt (page 44)

1 (2- to 3-pound [0.9- to 1.4-kg]) whole beef skirt, trimmed of fat and membranes

1 red bell pepper, halved and seeded

1 green bell pepper, halved and seeded

1 large onion, cut into 8 wedges

4 tablespoons (56 g) butter, melted and flavored with a minced garlic clove, optional

Warm flour tortillas

Lime wedges for garnish

1 The night before you plan to barbecue, prepare the orange marinade, combining the orange juice, chopped onion, 4 tablespoons (60 g) melted butter, Worcestershire sauce, dry mustard, and 1 tablespoon (10 g) Red Dirt rub in a shallow dish. Add the skirt steak to the marinade, cover, and refrigerate overnight, turning occasionally if needed to saturate the meat.

2 The next day, drain and discard the marinade from the skirt steak. Let the steak sit at room temperature for about 30 minutes. Arrange the onion wedges and bell pepper halves on a small mesh grill rack.

3 Prepare the smoker for barbecuing, bringing the temperature to 225°F to 250°F (107°C to 120°C).

4 Transfer the skirt steak and rack of vegetables to the smoker. Cook for approximately 45 minutes until the meat is browned and cooked through to at least medium doneness. Remove the vegetables when tender.

5 If your smoker has a separate grill area for cooking directly over a fire or if you have another grill handy, move the meat there and sear it for 1 to 2 minutes per side. This step adds a pleasant crispy exterior texture but isn't necessary for flavor. Alternatively, smoke the skirt steak for about 15 minutes longer.

6 If desired, brush the skirt steak with 4 tablespoons (60 ml) of melted garlic butter. Slice the skirt steak very thinly on the diagonal against the grain. Slice the vegetables and serve both with the tortillas and squeezes of lime.

Cooking beef cheeks, cachete, *is a great way to get classic barbacoa flavor without committing to the traditional full steer's head in a pit in the ground. You can find beef cheeks at a butcher shop or a supermarket that caters to a Hispanic or Latino clientele. The cheeks have a deeply beefy favor and become super tender and almost silky when slow cooked. They are full of collagen, which helps keep them moist while cooking. Just make sure to smoke them until the meat shreds easily. It will remain somewhat sticky. And that pit in the ground and whole cow's head idea? Well, if you really want to try that, the best instructions and photos I've seen are at jesspryles.com.*

DEL RIO CACHETE BARBACOA

PREPARATION TIME: 15 MINUTES

COOKING TIME: ABOUT 5 HOURS

SERVES 6 OR MORE

CACHETE RUB

2 tablespoons (12 g) coarsely ground
   black pepper

1 tablespoon (19 g) kosher salt
   or coarse sea salt

2 teaspoons granulated garlic

1 teaspoon ground cumin

3 (2-pound [905-g]) beef cheeks,
   trimmed of silverskin and
   surface fat

1 small onion, finely chopped

Wedges from 2 or more limes

Warm corn or flour tortillas

Your favorite salsa

1   Combine the black pepper, salt, granulated garlic, and cumin in a small bowl. Pat the rub all over the beef cheeks. Let sit at room temperature for about 30 minutes.

2   Prepare the smoker for barbecuing, bringing the temperature to 250°F to 275°F (120°C to 140°C).

3   Transfer the beef cheeks to the smoker, placing them directly on the grate, and cook for about 5 hours. Smoke until the meat is well done and an instant-read thermometer inserted horizontally into the meat reads 200°F to 205°F (93°C to 96°C). Shred the meat finely with a pair of forks and discard any fat. Mix any drippings back into it the meat. Stir in the onion.

4   Serve hot, squeezing lime wedges over the meat and then piling it into tortillas. Offer salsa on the side and enjoy.

Smoke Rings

The smoke ring, or layer of pink you find just under the surface of most slow-smoked meat, is not an indication of undercooking. When the pink runs from the outside in, as it does in barbecue, it results from the smoking process and becomes more distinct as the meat gets well done. When the pink runs from the center out, like in a rare steak, the meat is cooked less thoroughly than possible. Barbecue authorities often judge smoked food initially by the depth of the smoke ring, hoping to find something heftier than a thin red line.

"Barbecuing is only incidentally cooking, and barbecuists avoid, as much as possible, confusing the two. Barbecue is play—serious, mind-concentrating, important, risk-running, even exhausting . . . anything, in fact, except a chore. In real barbecue there's no washing up."

—JOHN THORNE,
SIMPLE COOKING NEWSLETTER, 1988

Few main dishes dazzle guests like beef tenderloin. This is an easy but elegant version, flavored simply with garlic, salt, and pepper and then soaked in smoke and seared off just before serving for a crusty surface. Ask for a center-cut section of the tenderloin for the most even thickness, which makes for more even cooking. It really doesn't require this zipped-up version of the classic French béarnaise sauce, but it's easier to make than you might guess and sure good with it. Just have all of the sauce ingredients ready to go when it's time to prepare it.

PEPPERED BEEF TENDERLOIN WITH JALAPEÑO BÉARNAISE

PREPARATION TIME: 30 MINUTES

COOKING TIME: ABOUT 1¼ HOURS

SERVES 6

3 tablespoons (30 g) Dalmatian Rub
　(page 43)

2 teaspoons granulated garlic

1 (2-pound [905-g]) beef tenderloin,
　preferably center cut

1 cup (235 ml) beef stock

½ cup (120 ml) dry red wine

2 tablespoons (30 ml) olive oil
　or vegetable oil, divided

JALAPEÑO BÉARNAISE

¼ cup (60 ml) white wine vinegar

1 pickled jalapeño, seeded and
　minced,

1 tablespoon (15 ml) jalapeño
　pickling liquid from the jar

1 large shallot, minced

1 tablespoon (4 g) chopped fresh
　tarragon, or 1½ teaspoons dried
　tarragon

16 tablespoons (225 g) salted butter,
　cut into several chunks

2 large egg yolks

1 tablespoon (15 ml) water

Kosher salt and freshly ground
　black pepper

1　Combine the Dalmatian Rub and granulated garlic in a small bowl. Pat the rub all over the tenderloin. Cover the tenderloin and let it sit at room temperature for about 30 minutes.

2　For the mop, combine the stock, wine, and 1 tablespoon (15 ml) oil in a saucepan
and warm over low heat.

3　Prepare the smoker for barbecuing, bringing the temperature to 225°F to 250°F (107°C to 120°C).

4　Transfer the tenderloin to the smoker, placing it directly on the grate, and cook for 1 to 1¼ hours, mopping every 20 minutes in a wood-burning pit, or as appropriate for your style of smoker. The meat is ready when the internal temperature reaches 135°F to 140°F (57°C to 60°C). Be careful not to overcook, since tenderloin is best rare to medium rare, and you still need to sear off the tenderloin to finish.

5　In a heavy skillet, heat the remaining 1 tablespoon oil over high heat. Sear the meat on all sides, about 30 seconds per side, including the ends. The final internal temperature should be 140°F to 145°F (60°C to 63°C). Let rest for 10 minutes or so while you make the Jalapeño Béarnaise sauce.

6　Combine in a small saucepan the vinegar, jalapeño, pickling liquid, shallot, and tarragon. Bring to a boil over medium heat and reduce to about 2 tablespoons (28 ml) liquid, about 5 minutes. Set aside. Melt the butter in another small pan. Combine the egg yolks and 1 tablespoon (25 ml) water in a blender and combine for a few seconds. Remove the blender top's insert and, with the blender running on medium speed, slowly pour in the warm butter in a very thin stream. Continue blending for a minute or so until the sauce is creamy. Pour it into a bowl and stir in the jalapeño-shallot mixture. Adjust seasoning with salt and black pepper as needed. Serve right away.

The magnificent rib roast, or prime rib, is essentially a bunch of rib-eye steaks just waiting to be sliced. Treat yourself once to a USDA Prime prime rib and you will never go back. In this preparation, the roast is cooked over a higher temperature than I recommend typically, but it works for this bigger cut. You want only to cook this to medium rare.

SMOKE-ROASTED STANDING RIB ROAST

PREPARATION TIME: 30 MINUTES

COOKING TIME: 2 TO 2½ HOURS

SERVES 8

¾ cup (125 g) Dalmatian Rub (page 43)

1 tablespoon plus 1 teaspoon (12 g) garlic powder

1 tablespoon plus 1 teaspoon (4 g) crumbled dried oregano

1 (7- to 8-pound [3.2-to 3.6-kg]) 4-rib rib roast (prime rib)

1   Combine the Dalmatian Rub, garlic powder, and oregano in a small bowl and mix well. Massage the dry rub all over the roast. Let sit at room temperature while getting the smoker ready.

2   Prepare the smoker for barbecuing, bringing the temperature to 300°F to 325°F (150°C to 170°C).

3   Before cooking, take the internal temperature of the meat, deep in the roast's center, with an instant-read thermometer. The temperature should be nearing 40°F (4°C), considered the high end of the safe range for beef to sit out unrefrigerated. If the temperature of the roast is more than a couple of degrees below 40°F (4°C), plan to extend the cooking time by a few minutes.

4   Transfer the prime rib to the smoker, placing it directly on the grate, fattier side up. Plan on a total cooking time of 2 to 2½ hours. After 1½ hours, check the internal temperature, deep in the roast's center again, to gauge the rest of the cooking time. I prefer to take the roast off when it is in the rare to medium-rare range, 120°F to 130°F (49°C to 54°C). Please don't cook it beyond 140°F (60°C), the high side of medium.

5   Let the prime rib roast sit for 20 minutes. Be sure to show it off to your guests! Carve into thick slices and serve.

Smoked burgers blow away the grilled competition. You can simply coat the burgers in salt and pepper before cooking, but I like to up the Southwest flavor with Chile Dust rub. If you want to serve them Tex-Mex style, ladle on your favorite queso rather than sliced cheese.

A SMOKIN' BURGER

PREPARATION TIME: 30 MINUTES

COOKING TIME: 45 MINUTES

SERVES 4

¼ cup (40 g) Chile Dust (page 45)

2 pounds (900 g) freshly ground beef
   (80/20 ratio of fat to lean)

Sturdy burger buns

Mayonnaise, ketchup, mustard,
   red-ripe tomato slices, dill pickle
   slices, crisp iceberg lettuce leaves

1   Prepare the smoker for barbecuing, bringing the temperature to 225°F to 250°F (107°C to 120°C).

2   In a large bowl, combine the Chile Dust and ground beef. Don't mix any longer than needed just to combine it evenly. Form the mixture into four patties about ½ inch (1.3 cm) thick.

3   Transfer the patties to the smoker, placing them directly on the grate. Cook until done at least to medium with a temperature of 160°F (71°C), about for 45 minutes.

4   Serve on the buns with your choice of condiments and enjoy right away.

VARIATION: Brisket Burgers. *Make your burger mixture with 1½ pounds (680 g) ground beef and ½ pound (255 g) finely chopped barbecued brisket.*

Virtually all of the well-known sausages of German- and Eastern European–influenced Central Texas are filled with pork, at least some pork. Not so in the state's southeast corner, where the African-American developed beef link is king. In this neck of the woods, these are a much more popular way to treat brisket than smoking it whole. Patillo's Bar-B-Que in Beaumont, opened in 1912, gets the credit for creating this type of sausage, made throughout the area from down in Galveston and up to Jasper. The meat's typically coarse-ground, it's plenty juicy, and those juices should run red. You'll need a meat grinder or the meat grinding attachment for a stand mixer. If beef casings for sausage are impossible to find, you can substitute pork casings but the links will likely come out somewhat more thin.

BEAUMONT BEEF LINKS

PREPARATION TIME: 2 HOURS PLUS OVERNIGHT REFRIGERATION

COOKING TIME: 2 TO 2 ¼ HOURS

MAKES ABOUT 2 DOZEN SAUSAGES, SERVING 12 OR MORE

6 pounds (2.7 kg) untrimmed ground beef brisket
1 cup (235 ml) very cold water
¼ cup (17 g) nonfat powdered milk
12 plump garlic cloves, minced
2 tablespoons (38 g) kosher salt or coarse sea salt
1 tablespoon (8 g) chili powder
1 tablespoon (4 g) dried red pepper flakes
1 tablespoon (7 g) sweet paprika
1 tablespoon (5 g) ground cayenne
Vegetable oil
5 yards (4.6 m) beef sausage casings

1   At least the evening before you plan to barbecue the sausages, grind the brisket using the coarse-grind blade of a meat grinder. Place in a bowl and mix in the water thoroughly. Then, mix in the powdered milk, garlic, salt, chili powder, red pepper flakes, cayenne, and paprika. Refrigerate covered overnight.

2   Prepare the casings, soaking them in several changes of water over several hours. Then, flush the casings with cool water to remove remaining salt.

3   With the stuffing attachment of a meat grinder, stuff the cold mixture into the casings, making links about 1½ inch (3.8 cm) thick by about 8 inches (20 cm) long. The casings should feel full but not jam-packed. Bend each sausage into a round and tie the two ends together with kitchen twine.

4   If you end up with any air bubbles, prick the casing in those spots with a needle. The sausage is ready to barbecue, but can be refrigerated for several days or frozen for at least a month.

5   Prepare the smoker for barbecuing, bringing the temperature to 200°F to 225°F (93°C to 107°C). Rub the sausages lightly with the oil.

6   Transfer the links to the smoker and cook for 2 to 2¼ hours or until the skins look completely ready to pop and the internal temperature of a link is 160°F (71°C). Serve hot. Some folks slice the links to eat them. Others squeeze the filling out of the casings, discarding the casings. Enjoy, however you choose to devour them.

She's Australian, but she got to Texas as fast as she could. Based in Austin, Jess Pryles (jesspryles.com) has the most brilliantly named book and barbecue-related products— Hardcore Carnivore. It makes me smile every time I say it. She's an expert in live-fire cooking. Until this recipe came out in her inspiring newsletter, it never occurred to me to think of beef as a source for bacon. As Jess says, "It's not just piggies that have bellies though. Steers have some mighty belly meat that transforms into incredibly flavorful bacon." She likes to point out that the flavor might spark some taste memories for those of us old enough to have grown up eating French fries cooked in beef tallow. There are three steps but none is difficult, once you procure a portion of a beef belly, which is called beef navel in the world of butchery.

JESS PRYLES'S BEEF BACON

PREPARATION TIME: 4 TO 6 DAYS

COOKING TIME: ABOUT 3 HOURS

SERVES 6

Curing Mix

⅓ cup (67 g) sugar

3 tablespoons (56 g) kosher salt
    or coarse sea salt

2 tablespoons (12 g) finely ground
    black pepper

2 teaspoons ground sweet paprika

1 teaspoon pink curing salt

3½- to 4-pound (1.6 to 1.8 kg)
    section beef navel (belly)

For Making This Bacon
You will need some pink curing salt, also known as Prague Powder #1. The curing salt is designed to prevent food-borne illness in cured items like bacon or sausage. It is available at specialty grocers and easy to find online and should not be left out. Neither should you replace it with additional kosher or sea salt. Smoke with hickory or mesquite if you have a choice.

1   To cure the beef navel, combine the sugar, kosher salt, black pepper, paprika, and curing salt. Massage the cure mixture into all sides of the beef navel. It must be well-coated. Place the belly in a large plastic bag, making sure to get as much of the cure mixture into the bag with the beef as you can manage.

2   Transfer the bag to the refrigerator. If you have space, it's a good idea to place a baking sheet or other dish under it, in case of any unexpected drips. The beef needs to cure for 3 to 5 days. Once daily, massage the liquid that accumulates in the bag back into the beef and turn over the bag.

3   After the curing process is complete, discard the bag and rinse off the beef. Dry with paper towels. Return the uncovered belly to the refrigerator on a rack, again over a baking sheet, and let it dry out for 1 day or night.

4   Prepare the smoker for barbecuing, bringing the temperature to about 200°F (93°C).

5   Transfer the belly to the smoker and smoke until it reaches an internal temperature of 150°F (66°C). Let the belly sit at room temperature until cool. Then wrap in plastic and refrigerate until cold at least 2 hours.

6   To prepare the bacon, cut the number of slices you wish to fry as thinly as possible, which is easier to do after when the bacon is thoroughly chilled. The bacon will keep up to 2 weeks in the refrigerator.

7   Cook the bacon slices, starting with a cold skillet over medium-low heat. Cook several minutes until crisp on both sides. Drain on paper towels and serve right away as you would any bacon.

With all of the protein-focused diets popular today, beef jerky has gone from an Old West preservation method to the food of hipsters. Who woulda thunk it? This barbecue version has flavor rather than longevity in mind.

CHILE-RUBBED BEEF JERKY

PREPARATION TIME: 30 MINUTES,
PLUS 30 MINUTES IN THE FREEZER

COOKING TIME: 1¾ TO 2 HOURS

SERVES 6 TO 8 AS A SNACK

1 to 1¼ pounds (455 to 570 g)
   top round steak
¼ cup plus 2 tablespoons (60 g)
   Red Dirt (page 44)

1   About 2 hours before you plan to barbecue, place the round steak in the freezer to make slicing easier. After 30 to 40 minutes, remove the steak and slice it across the grain as thinly as possible. Transfer the slices of steak to a baking sheet, laying them out somewhat loosely.

2   Sprinkle all of the Red Dirt rub over the steak. Rub it with your fingers, heaping up the slices as needed to coat all of them evenly with rub. Separate the slices, laying them out more or less in a single layer. (If a baking sheet is too large for your smoker, make a tray out of heavy-duty aluminum foil in a more appropriate size. Try to keep the steak slices laid out neatly still.)

3   Prepare the smoker for barbecuing, bringing the temperature to 200°F to 220°F (93°C to 104°C).

4   Transfer the baking sheet to the smoker, placing it in the coolest part. Cook until dried, about 1¾ to 2 hours. Let cool before serving standing up in glasses for everyone to select slices as they wish. Refrigerate any leftovers.

CHAPTER 6

PORK, PLUS LAMB, GOAT, AND GAME, OH MY

For all the focus on beef barbecue, Texans are cooking up plenty of other meats too. Ribs and pork sausage have been the traditional go-to non-beef Q, but they're joined these days by pork steaks cut from the shoulder as well as full pork shoulder for pulling. Lamb has a history in barbacoa in South Texas, and Central Texas has been the home of goat barbecue. And game, whether venison or bison, can show up on the table as often as these other meats. Enjoy the diversity.

Miss Tootsie and Miss Chloe

My personal barbecue hero is the spry octogenarian pitmaster at Snow's BBQ in Lexington, Tootsie Tomanetz. She barbecues a terrific beef brisket and link sausages but is known for a more unusual cut as well: the pork butt (or shoulder) steak. In 2009, not too long after Texas Monthly declared Snow's (a place only open for half a day each week) the best barbecue in the entire state, we arranged a family barbecue field trip from Austin. The place opened on Saturday mornings at 8 a.m., but we knew we would need to be in line some 30 minutes to an hour in advance of the opening. Chloe, our youngest grandchild, was five and, when rousted from bed at 5 a.m., not as thrilled with this trip as she had been in the theoretical discussions about it in the days prior to hitting the road. After arrival, we were challenged with waking Chloe and her two siblings again. Finally, with everyone vertical, we stood in line but also watched the preparations of the barbecue by Miss Tootsie under a covered open-air shed of sorts. Eventually, we snagged our barbecue and a table inside. We were surprised and delighted that the still-sleepy Chloe thought to put together a sandwich with some of our bread, sliced pork steak, and sauce, placed it on a napkin, and announced that she was taking it to Miss Tootsie. She figured—rightly—that Miss Tootsie had been up for even more hours than us and really should have something to eat. Miss Tootsie accepted the smooshed little sandwich with the graciousness of a queen. I still smile when I think of Chloe's determination and kindness.

A cut of pork shoulder, these steaks are inspired by the remarkable version at Snow's in Lexington. Snow's is only open one day a week, so it's good to know how to make something similar at home. If you'd like a sauce accompaniment, I'd opt for one with a decent hit of mustard.

PORK BUTT STEAKS

PREPARATION TIME: 15 MINUTES, PLUS OVERNIGHT REFRIGERATION

COOKING TIME: ABOUT 3 HOURS

SERVES 6 TO 8

¼ cup plus 2 tablespoons (62 g) Dalmatian Rub (page 43), divided

1 tablespoon (10 g) granulated garlic

4 (2- to 2½-pound [0.9- to 1.1-kg]) bone-in pork shoulder steaks, cut at least 1½ inch (3.8 cm) thick

1 batch Mustard Mop for Pork and Chicken (page 48)

1   The night before you plan to barbecue, combine the Dalmation Rub and granulated garlic and massage all but 1 tablespoon (10 g) of the rub into the pork steaks. Transfer the pork steaks to a plastic bag and refrigerate them overnight.

2   The next day, remove the pork steaks from the refrigerator. Let the pork steaks sit at room temperature for about 45 minutes.

3   Prepare the mop, if needed, and keep warm while barbecuing.

4   Prepare the smoker for barbecuing, bringing the temperature to 225°F to 250°F (107°C to 120°C).

5   Transfer the pork steaks to the smoker, placing them directly on the grate, and cook for about 3 hours until approximately 200°F (93°C) and just short of fall-apart tender. Mop the pork steaks about once an hour in a wood-burning pit or as appropriate for your style of smoker.

6   Remove the pork steaks from the smoker and let them sit briefly. The meat is typically sliced away from the bone, rather than pulled, but do what works best for you. However you serve it, make sure each portion has some of the darker exterior meat and some of the softer interior meat.

In today's Texas, barbecue takes about a thousand guises. I remember it was completely common a few decades ago to come across "barbecue" signs at joints in Central Texas, in particular, which meant beef generally in one or two forms, and then separately listed would be "spare ribs" or "spareribs." This is a saucy version of ribs, inspired by the African-American barbecue traditions of eastern Texas. I cook them in a style called 3-2-1, which involves 3 hours naked, 2 hours "foiled", and 1 hour naked. Use hickory as the wood for cooking, if possible.

EAST TEXAS SPARE RIBS

PREPARATION TIME: 45 MINUTES

COOKING TIME: ABOUT 6 HOURS

SERVES 4 TO 6

EAST TEXAS RUB

3 tablespoons (18 g) finely ground
　black pepper

2 tablespoons (14 g) sweet paprika

2 tablespoons (30 g) packed light
　or dark brown sugar

2 teaspoons kosher salt or coarse
　sea salt

½ teaspoon ground cayenne

2 full slabs pork spare ribs,
　preferably 3 pounds (1.4 kg) each
　or slightly less, cut St. Louis style,
　trimmed of the chine bone and
　brisket flap

1 cup (235 ml) Vinegar Spritz (page 49)

EAST TEXAS BARBECUE SAUCE

1 (8-ounce [235-ml]) can
　tomato sauce

¼ cup (85 g) molasses

¼ cup (60 ml) cider vinegar

2 teaspoons finely ground
　black pepper

1 teaspoon onion powder

1 teaspoon Tabasco sauce
　or other Louisiana hot sauce

½ teaspoon kosher salt or coarse
　sea salt

1 If your butcher hasn't stripped the shiny silver membrane on the ribs' concave side, remove it. First, slip a butter knife or paring knife under one end of the membrane. Move the knife back and forth enough that you can get a couple of fingers in between the membrane and the meat. Once you've worked your fingers underneath far enough to grip the membrane, pull slowly, trying to take the whole membrane off in one piece. It's slippery, so you may want to use a paper towel to help pull it off.

2 To marinate overnight, combine the black pepper, paprika, brown sugar, salt, and cayenne in a small bowl. Apply the rub evenly to the ribs. Place the ribs in a plastic bag or on a baking sheet and then covered with plastic wrap, and refrigerate.

3 The next day, take the ribs from the refrigerator. Let them sit uncovered at room temperature for 30 to 40 minutes. Prepare the smoker for barbecuing, bringing the temperature to 225°F to 250°F (107°C to 120°C).

4 Transfer the ribs to the smoker, placing them directly on the grate. Cook the ribs for a total of about 6 hours. In the first 3 hours turn the ribs over and rotate from end to end every hour and spray with the vinegar spritz. After 3 hours, wrap each rack in heavy-duty aluminum foil and return to the smoker for the next 2 hours for the pork to steam and simmer. You don't need to add wood to the smoker during this time unless the wood is your cooking medium, as with a log-burning pit. Unwrap the ribs and return them to the smoker. Add enough wood for cooking 1 hour more.

5 While the ribs are cooking, prepare the sauce. Combine the tomato sauce, molasses, vinegar, 2 teaspoons black pepper, onion powder, Tabasco, and salt in a medium saucepan. Cook over medium heat for 10 to 15 minutes, just long enough for the flavors to meld together.

6 In the last 30 minutes of cooking, brush the ribs thickly with the sauce. Just before removing them from the grill, baste once more with the sauce. The ribs should be very well done at this point with meat that comes off the bone very easily when tugged. Slice into individual ribs and serve with any additional sauce on the side, if you like.

Of all the serious barbecue meats that you can cook in a gas grill modified for indirect cooking with added wood, I find back ribs come out the very best. There's not even much fiddling around with them. (Of course, they're also great if you can prepare them in a dedicated smoker.) These get a generous coating of dry rub and a few spritzes of inexpensive balsamic vinegar during the cook. While the wood choice doesn't make a huge difference, I've found that I particularly like a combination of mesquite and cherry on these. You can serve a couple of choices of sauces with the ribs, warmed if you like.

BACK RIBS

PREPARATION TIME: ABOUT
45 MINUTES

COOKING TIME: ABOUT 3 HOURS

SERVES 6

RIB RUB

3 tablespoons (18 g) coarsely ground
   black pepper

3 tablespoons (21 g) sweet paprika

1½ tablespoons (28 g) kosher salt or
   coarse sea salt

1½ tablespoons (18 g)
   turbinado sugar

1½ teaspoons dry mustard

1½ teaspoons chili powder

2 tablespoons (22 g) yellow mustard,
   divided, optional

2 racks pork back ribs, preferably
   12 bones and about 1½ pounds
   (680 kg) each

Inexpensive balsamic vinegar

1   If your butcher hasn't stripped the shiny silver membrane on the ribs' concave side, remove it. First, slip a butter knife or paring knife under one end of the membrane. Move the knife back and forth enough that you can get a couple of fingers in between the membrane and the meat. Once you've worked your fingers underneath far enough to grip the membrane, pull slowly, trying to take the whole membrane off in one piece. It's slippery, so you may want to use a paper towel to help pull it off.

2   Combine the black pepper, paprika, salt, sugar, dry mustard, and chili powder in a bowl. Set aside 2 tablespoons (20 g) of the rub. If you wish, slather each rib rack with about 1 tablespoon (11 g) yellow mustard before adding the rub. Divide the rub equally between the racks and massage into the ribs. Let sit at room temperature for about 30 minutes.

3   Prepare the smoker for barbecuing, bringing the temperature to 250°F to 275°F (120°C to 140°C).

4   Transfer the ribs to the smoker, placing them directly on the grate. Cook the ribs for approximately 3 hours. Once an hour, flip them over and turn them around from end to end and spritz them several times with the vinegar. After the second hour and after spritzing with vinegar, sprinkle the top of each rack with 1 tablespoon (10 g) of the remaining 2 tablespoons of rub.

5   When the slabs are ready, they should be deeply brown and the meat will bend easily between the ribs. If you pull the rib racks out with tongs, the ends will sag moderately. Slice the racks into individual ribs and serve.

VARIATION: Sauced Ribs. *If you want saucy ribs, brush your choice of sauce on the ribs about 45 minutes before you plan to remove the meat from the smoker. Repeat the step about 5 minutes before the ribs are ready.*

Remember when pork belly was reserved for makin' bacon? This delectable version of burnt ends seems like such an obvious idea that you'd think it must have been around for decades. Well, someone might have been cooking them up in their backyard, but it was Travis and Emma Heim's Fort Worth–based Heim Barbecue that began serving them and changed the landscape of barbecue all over the state. Even that bastion of classic Texas Q, Kreutz's, has put them on the menu.

PORK BELLY BURNT ENDS WITH JALAPEÑO JELLY GLAZE

PREPARATION TIME: 30 MINUTES, PLUS 4 TO 12 HOURS' REFRIGERATION

COOKING TIME: ABOUT 3½ HOURS

SERVES 8 OR MORE

¾ cup (130 g) Pork Rib and Belly Rub (page 46)

1 batch Citrus-Mustard Mop for Beef, Pork, and Chicken (page 48)

1 (3½- to 4-pound [1.6- to 1.8-kg]) uncooked section pork belly, preferably with skin on and without rib bones

½ cup (112 g) jalapeño jelly

1   Before you plan to smoke the pork belly, pack all but 1 tablespoon (6.3 g) of the rub over the meaty side of the pork belly. Place in a large plastic bag and refrigerate, skin-side down, for at least 4 hours and up to overnight.

2   Prepare the smoker for barbecuing, bringing the temperature to 200°F to 225°F (93°C to 107°C).

3   Prepare the mop, if needed, and keep the mixture warm over low heat while barbecuing.

4   Place the pork belly, skin-side up, on a rimmed baking sheet. Transfer the baking sheet to the smoker and cook for about 3 hours, mopping about once an hour in a wood-burning pit, or as appropriate in your style of smoker. The pork belly is ready when it is cooked to well done, approximately 175°F (79°C). Be careful with the hot liquid pork fat. Keep the smoker going.

5   Let the meat sit at room temperature for about 15 minutes then slice off and discard the skin. Cut the meat into ½-inch (1.3-cm)–thick slices, or another size and shape if you wish. Reserve the baking sheet with its pork fat.

6   If the jalapeño jelly is too thick to brush on easily, add a little water to it. Brush the pork belly slices with the jelly and return them to the baking sheet. Transfer the baking sheet back to the smoker and cook for another 15 to 30 minutes until the jelly has melted and caramelized in places. Serve hot. (If you end up with leftovers, reheat the slices on a griddle or in a heavy skillet to crisp and heat through.)

Porking Out
Want to do something ridiculously awesome? My son-in-law JB Neale and his other backyard barbecue buddies frequently get a side of pork belly when they're planning to cook brisket, beef or pork ribs, or a pork shoulder or ham. The pork belly goes on a shelf above the main barbecue event and its fat drips down over the other food during the long cooking time.

With high-quality beef steaks such as rib-eye, strip, and porterhouse, I think grilling is the best method for cooking them over fire. With pork chops, though, I grill and smoke them about equally. Smoking isn't a lengthy project with something this small and tender, and it enhances the flavor tremendously. Use a heritage breed of pork, such as Duroc or Berkshire, if you can.

ESPRESSO-RUBBED PORK CHOPS

PREPARATION TIME: 15 MINUTES

COOKING TIME: 45 TO 55 MINUTES

SERVES 6

6 bone-in center-cut pork chops,
 ½ inch to ¾ inch (1.3 to 2 cm)
 thick
¼ cup (35 g) Jolt (page 46)
2 teaspoons vegetable oil

1   Massage the chops with the Jolt rub.

2   Prepare the smoker for barbecuing, bringing the temperature to 225°F to 250°F (107°C to 120°C).

3   Warm the oil in a heavy skillet over high heat. Quickly sear the chops on both sides and transfer to the smoker (without the skillet). Cook the chops 45 to 55 minutes until their internal temperature reaches 155°F (68°C) on an instant-read thermometer. Serve hot.

Don't judge until you've tasted it. Get a decent hunk of bologna to start with, and you'll be rewarded with magnificence and great memories of childhood. If you want to turn it into sandwiches, add some of the sauce you used for smoking and maybe some chowchow or chopped onions.

BARBECUED BOLOGNA

PREPARATION TIME: 45 MINUTES

COOKING TIME: 1½ HOURS

SERVES 6 TO 8

1 (2-pound [900-g]) chunk bologna

½ cup (120 ml) East Texas Molasses
   BBQ Sauce (page 141) or
   Sweet-Sour Honey-Mustard
   Barbecue Sauce (page 144) or
   another favorite barbecue sauce

1 tablespoon (15 ml) cider vinegar
   or white vinegar

1 Score the bologna ¼ (6 mm) deep with wide crisscrossed cuts. Mix the barbecue sauce with the vinegar to thin. Cover the bologna thoroughly with the thinned sauce. Let the bologna sit at room temperature for 20 to 30 minutes.

2 Prepare the smoker for barbecuing, bringing the temperature to 250°F to 275°F (120°C to 140°C).

3 Transfer the bologna to the smoker, placing it directly on the grate, and cook for about 1½ hours. The sauce will have caramelized on the bologna's surface. Serve sliced, warm or cold, as a sandwich if you like.

"You can make a real dingwilly of a dish of plain old bologna by pepping it up on the grill."

—WALTER JETTON,
WALTER JETTON'S LBJ BARBECUE COOK BOOK, 1965

There's a lot more pork being pulled around Texas than you might think. You can get a mustard-and-brown-sugar-rubbed version at Gatlin's BBQ in Houston or a beer-marinated version served at the Paulaner Brewery at Addison Oktoberfest. The boldness of Korean seasonings plays well to the Texas palate, so versions of this are popping up like bluebonnets during a Central Texas spring. Most of us who are home cooks will find barbecuing a pork butt a lot easier than a brisket, so what are you waiting for? You could top the sandwiches with store-bought kimchi if you like.

KOREAN PULLED PORK

PREPARATION TIME: 30 MINUTES, PLUS 2 HOURS' REFRIGERATION

COOKING TIME: ABOUT 6 HOURS

SERVES 6 TO 8

CARROT-RADISH RELISH

2 medium carrots, peeled, halved
   lengthwise, and sliced thin
1 bunch mild radishes, tops and tails
   trimmed and discarded, halved and
   sliced thin
¾ cup (175 ml) rice vinegar
½ cup (100 g) granulated sugar
½ teaspoon kosher salt or coarse
   sea salt

KOREAN SEASONING PASTE

¼ cup (60 ml) *ganjang* (Korean soy
   sauce) or other soy sauce
3 tablespoons (45 g) *gochujang*
   (Korean red pepper paste)
   or (45 ml) sriracha
3 cloves garlic, minced
1 tablespoon (15 ml) toasted
   sesame oil
1 tablespoon (15 g) packed light
   or dark brown sugar
1 (3½- to 4-pound [1.6- to 1.8-kg])
   section pork butt
6 to 8 large hamburger buns
Cilantro leaves or green onions
   (green and white portions) sliced in
   very thin rounds, optional

1 In a medium bowl, combine the carrots, radishes, rice vinegar, granulated sugar, and salt. Refrigerate for at least 2 hours.

2 Prepare the seasoning paste, mixing the *ganjang*, *gochujang*, garlic, sesame oil, and brown sugar together in a small bowl. Rub the paste all over the pork, getting it into the crevices of the meat. Let the meat sit at room temperature for about 30 minutes.

3 Prepare the smoker for barbecuing, bringing the temperature to 225°F to 250°F (107°C to 120°C).

4 Transfer the meat to the smoker, placing it directly on the grate, and smoke it for 4 hours. After 4 hours, wrap the pork in heavy-duty foil. Return the pork to the smoker (or you can also bring it in the house and put it in the oven). Unless wood is the cooking medium, as with a log-burning pit, you can stop adding wood to the smoker. Cook until the fall-apart stage, about 2 hours more.

5 Unwrap the pork and let it sit until it's cool enough to handle. Pull the pork apart into bite-size shreds, discarding fat, cartilage, and bone.

6 Make sandwiches with the pork, piling it high on the bun bottoms. Top with some of the drained carrot-radish relish, and, if you wish, a scattering of cilantro leaves, green onions, or both. Serve right away.

I love a great brat on its own, but it's fun to dress up the Central Texas favorite in various ways. Around the barbecue cook-off circuit, you find a lot of the widely available Johnsonville bratwurst being smoked. However, if you have access to a local meat market's version, they are likely to be spiced up a bit more assertively with nutmeg, coriander, and caraway. The pickled mustard seeds need to sit for at least 3 hours after their quick prep to soften, but you can make them days ahead, if you like. The seeds are a tasty accompaniment to any smoked or grilled sausage or a pastrami sandwich. Serve the bratwursts with Kraut Salad (page 58), Red, White, and Blue Potato Salad (page 159), or Tater Tot Casserole (page 160) for an Oktoberfest celebration.

BACON-WRAPPED BRATS WITH PICKLED MUSTARD SEEDS AND JALAPEÑOS

PREPARATION TIME: 30 MINUTES, PLUS 3 HOURS' STANDING TIME

COOKING TIME: 1¼ TO 1½ HOURS

SERVES 6 TO 8

PICKLED MUSTARD SEEDS

¼ cup plus 2 tablespoons (66 g) yellow mustard seeds

½ cup (120 ml) white vinegar

¼ cup (60 ml) water

2 tablespoons (26 g) granulated sugar

½ teaspoon kosher salt or coarse sea salt

12 (4- to 6-ounce [115- to 170-g]) uncooked bratwursts

12 slices uncooked bacon

¼ cup (26 g) sliced pickled jalapeño peppers, plus more to taste

1 Dump the mustard seeds into a small heatproof bowl. Combine the vinegar, water, sugar, and salt in a small saucepan and bring to a full rolling boil over high heat. Pour the liquid over the mustard seeds and let stand for at least 3 hours. Refrigerate in a covered container or use right away.

2 Prepare the smoker for barbecuing, bringing the temperature to 200°F to 225°F (93°C to 107°C).

3 Wrap each bratwurst as fully as possible with a bacon slice. Secure the bacon with toothpicks at the ends of the bratwurst.

4 Transfer the brats to the smoker, placing them directly on the grate, and cook until the bacon is brown and crisp and the brats have plumped, 1¼ to 1½ hours, depending on size.

5 Mix the jalapeños with mustard seeds, adding more to taste if you wish. Plate the brats and top each with a heaping tablespoon (15 g) or so of the mustard seed and jalapeño mixture. Enjoy right away.

Of course you can order a variety of fabulous Texas link sausages from the Central Texas meat markets that popularized this style, but it's pretty impressive to folks when you say you made them yourself. You'll need a meat grinder or the meat grinder attachment to a stand mixer for this.

CENTRAL TEXAS HOT LINKS

PREPARATION TIME: 2 HOURS,
PLUS OVERNIGHT REFRIGERATION

COOKING TIME: 2 TO 2½ HOURS

MAKES ABOUT 2 DOZEN SAUSAGES

4 pounds (1.8 kg) pork butt,
   untrimmed, cut into 2-inch (5 cm)
   cubes
2 pounds (900 g) beef chuck or
   round steak, untrimmed, cut into
   2-inch (5 cm) cubes
1 large onion, minced
6 cloves garlic, minced
1 to 2 tablespoons (4 to 8 g) *chile
   caribe* or other crushed dried
   medium-hot red chile
1 tablespoon (2 g) dried sage
1 tablespoon (19 g) kosher salt
   or coarse sea salt
1 tablespoon (6 g) coarsely ground
   black pepper
½ to 1 teaspoon ground cayenne
4 yards (3.7 m) hog sausage casings
Vegetable oil

TO PREPARE THE SAUSAGES

1 At least the evening before you plan to barbecue the sausages, grind the pork and beef together into a large bowl, using the coarse-grind blade of a meat grinder. Add the onion, garlic, *chile caribe*, sage, salt, black pepper, and cayenne. If you wish, grind the mixture again. Refrigerate, covered, overnight.

2 Prepare the casings, soaking them in several changes of water over an hour or so to eliminate the brine that preserves them. Run some water through each casing as well, to flush any remaining brine from the inside.

3 Using the stuffing attachment of a meat grinder or stand mixer, stuff the cold sausage mixture into the casings, making 1-inch (2.5 cm)–thick links about 5 inches (13 cm) long. With your fingers, twist the casing to create a link, and if you're the fastidious type, tie off the individual sausages with kitchen twine. Cut between the links. If you end up with any air bubbles, prick the casing in those spots with a needle. The sausage is ready to barbecue but can be refrigerated for several days or frozen for at least a month.

TO SMOKE THE SAUSAGES

4 Prepare the smoker for barbecuing, bringing the temperature to 200°F to 225°F (93°C to 107°C). Rub the sausages lightly but thoroughly with oil.

5 Transfer the sausage links to the smoker, placing them directly on the cooking grate. Cook until the skin balloons up and looks ready to pop, 2 to 2¼ hours. Cut one of the sausages open to check for doneness before serving them.

The Cajun country that spills over into Southeast Texas from Louisiana produces boudin *(or* boudain*) blanc, a link sausage of sorts, traditionally a pork and rice masterpiece eaten at all hours of the day. This boudin is called "blanc" to distinguish it from* boudin rouge, *a blood sausage rarely seen except at hog-butchering parties. If you don't want to go to all the work of making your own sausages, you can order several varieties of* boudin blanc *from cajungrocer. com and simply smoke them before you serve them. These days, you might come across a boudin in Texas flavored with Thai green or red curry or other nontraditional spices. Once you have the basics down, feel free to experiment with other flavorings.*

BOUDIN BLANC

PREPARATION TIME: 2 HOURS,
PLUS REFRIGERATION

COOKING TIME: ABOUT 45 MINUTES

MAKES ABOUT 2 DOZEN LINKS

FILLING

1 (2¾- to 3-pound [1.2- to 1.4-kg])
   section bone-in pork butt section

2 large onions, preferably yellow,
   chopped, divided

2 tablespoons (38 g) kosher salt
   or coarse sea salt, divided,
   plus more to taste

1 teaspoon dried thyme

4 to 6 ounces (115 to 170 g) fresh
   pork or chicken liver, optional

2 large cloves garlic, minced

6 cups (1.9 kg) freshly cooked rice
   (see Ingredient Tip)

1 cup (100 g) finely chopped green
   onions, tops included

1 fresh jalapeño, seeded and
   chopped

1 tablespoon (6 g) ground
   black pepper, plus more to taste

1½ teaspoons ground cayenne,
   plus more to taste

½ cup (120 ml) cream or
   half-and-half

4 yards (3.7 m) hog sausage casings

Vegetable oil

TO PREPARE THE BOUDIN

1   Cut the pork away from the bone into four or five similar-size chunks. Leave the fat on the meat. Place the pork and the bone in a large saucepan and cover with at least 2 inches (5 cm) of water. Add one-quarter of the chopped onions, 1 tablespoon (19 g) salt, and the thyme. Bring the mixture to a boil, skimming off any foam. Reduce the heat to a simmer and cook until very tender, about 1 ½ hours.

2   If you are using either the pork or chicken liver, place it in another saucepan and cover with at least 1 inch (2.5 cm) of water. Bring to a boil, skimming off any foam. Reduce the heat to a simmer and cook 1 hour. Drain the liver, discarding the water.

3   When the pork butt chunks are ready, remove them from the cooking liquid. Strain the liquid and reserve it. You will want 2 cups (475 ml) of liquid. If you have more, return the liquid to the pan and reduce it over high heat until you have 2 cups (475 ml). If you have less than 2 cups (475 ml), add enough water to measure the proper amount.

4   Working in batches, use a meat grinder (with a medium-grind disk) or a food processor to grind or finely chop the pork (still with the fat), liver, if using, remaining onions, and garlic. Transfer the mixture to a large bowl. Stir in 1 tablespoon (19 g) salt and the rice, green onions, jalapeño, black pepper, and cayenne. Pour in the cream and 1 cup (235 ml) cooking liquid and mix it in well. You want the filling to be moist but not runny. Add more or all of the cooking liquid as needed to get the proper consistency. To check the season- ing, cook up a tablespoon (15 g) or so of the mixture in a small skillet. The final flavors will meld further, but now is the time to add more salt, black pepper, or cayenne to taste. Chill the filling for at least 1 hour and up to a day.

5   Prepare the casings while the filling cools, soaking them in several changes of water over an hour or so to eliminate the brine that preserves them. Run some water through each casing as well, to flush any remaining brine from inside.

6   Leave the boudin filling in the refrigerator until just before you plan to stuff it into the casings. Using the stuffing attachment of a meat grinder or stand mixer, stuff the fillings into the casings. Work quickly to keep the fat from softening, which makes the mixture harder to stuff evenly. You should be able to make 1½ to 2 dozen sausages about 1 inch (2.5 cm) in diameter and 5 inches (13 cm) in length. With your fingers, twist the casings to form links and, if you're the fastidious type, tie off the individual sausages with kitchen twine. Cut between the links. If you end up with any air bubbles, prick the casing in those spots with a needle. (You can proceed to the next step and poach the boudin at this point or cover and refrigerate them for up to one additional day.)

7   To poach the boudin, bring a large pot of hot water to a simmer and add the boudin. Adjust the heat to keep the water at just a bare simmer, showing only an occasional breaking bubble. Cook for about 15 minutes. (Some or all of the boudin can be cooled briefly and then wrapped and refrigerated, to smoke in the next day or two. Freeze it if you won't be able to smoke it until a later time.)

TO SMOKE THE BOUDIN

1   Shortly before you plan to serve the boudin, prepare the smoker for barbecuing, bringing the temperature to 200°F to 225°F (93°C to 107°C).

2   Coat the boudin lightly but completely with vegetable oil. Arrange the boudin in a smokeproof pan or baking sheet. Transfer the pan to the smoker and cook for 30 to 45 minutes until the casings have swelled up like balloons around the boudin. Serve the boudin hot. Some people eat the boudin with the casing on. Most folks, however, squeeze the soft filling from the casing into their mouths—a casual, messy method that's delightfully effective.

Little lamb rib chops have a lengthy bone. Lamb loin chops, which resemble teeny T-bone steaks, can be used for this too, but you'll want to plate them and serve with a knife and fork.

ONE-BITE LAMB CHOPS

PREPARATION TIME: 15 MINUTES

COOKING TIME: 30 TO 40 MINUTES

SERVES 4 OR 6

LAMB RUB

2 teaspoons dried oregano

2 teaspoons ground cumin

1 teaspoon kosher salt or coarse sea salt

1 teaspoon finely ground black pepper

½ teaspoon granulated garlic

12 frenched lamb rib chops

1   Prepare the rub, mixing the oregano, cumin, salt, black pepper, and granulated garlic together in a small bowl. Massage the lamb chops with the rub.

2   Prepare the smoker for barbecuing, bringing the temperature to 225°F to 250°F (107°C to 120°C).

3   Transfer the chops to the smoker and put them directly on the grate. Cook them to your desired doneness, about 30 to 40 minutes. Serve two or three to a plate, leaning them against each other, with bones upward.

This South Texas–style dish would traditionally be wrapped in maguey leaves and cooked in an earthen pit. A bone-in leg of lamb stands in for a whole lamb or lamb's head. Serve with tortillas and salsa.

LEG OF LAMB BARBACOA

PREPARATION TIME: 30 MINUTES, PLUS OVERNIGHT REFRIGERATION

COOKING TIME: ABOUT 2½ HOURS

SERVES 6 TO 8

BARBACOA PASTE

½ medium onion, chopped

10 cloves garlic

3 tablespoons (45 ml) mezcal (preferably) or tequila

2 teaspoons kosher salt or coarse sea salt

¼ cup (60 ml) good-but-not-great olive oil

1 (5-pound [2.3-kg]) boned leg of lamb

Warm flour or corn tortillas, for serving

Roasted Salsa Verde (page 146) or another favorite salsa, for serving

1   The night before you plan to barbecue, prepare the seasoning paste. In a food processor, blend the onion, garlic, mezcal, salt, and olive oil. I like to leave just a bit of texture to the mixture. Rub the lamb with the paste, wrap it in plastic, and refrigerate overnight.

2   The next day, prepare the smoker for barbecuing, bringing the temperature to 225°F to 250°F (107°C to 120°C).

3   Transfer the lamb to the smoker, directly on the grate. Cook for about 2½ hours (or 30 to 35 minutes per pound [455 g]) until the internal temperature reaches 145°F to 150°F (63°C to 66°C, medium rare).

4   Remove the lamb from the smoker and let it rest for 10 minutes. Slice and serve with tortillas and salsa.

"When you sit at a common table and share your enthusiasm for great smoked meat, tangy sauce, or juicy sausage with the people you meet, you become a part of a community of barbecue lovers. And that's what American barbecue culture is really all about."

—ROBB WALSH,
TEXAS HIGHWAYS, JULY 2013

The towns of Brady and Goldthwaite, pretty much smack-dab in the center of Texas, are both big centers for raising goats for mohair, and some goats make their way into the barbecue pit. Both places host goat cook-offs, in which hundreds of teams compete. Visitors can get a taste of goat too, which tends to be rather like lean beef. Back in the early 1990s, I interviewed the gentleman who oversaw the barbecuing of some 150 goats for the public lunch during the Brady World Championship Goat Cook-Off. I met his entire family, and not one of them would actually eat the barbecued goat. That would sure get my goat. For home barbecuing, I suggest using a young goat, or kid, usually referred to in Texas by its Spanish name, cabrito. Supermarkets like HEB and Fiesta Market often have cabrito, though it's best to check in advance. Butchers can usually point you in the right direction too. I like using an herb paste to help keep the lean meat moist.

CABRITO VERDE

PREPARATION TIME: 1½ HOURS, PLUS OVERNIGHT REFRIGERATION

COOKING TIME: 3 TO 4 HOURS

SERVES 6 TO 8

HERB PASTE

2½ cups (70 g) fresh sage leaves

½ cup (14 g) fresh rosemary leaves

1 head garlic, peeled

2 teaspoons kosher salt or coarse
   sea salt

1½ cups (355 ml) good-but-not-great
   olive oil

1 (10- to 12-pound [4.5- to 5.4-kg])
   cabrito, quartered by the butcher

MOP

2 cups (475 ml) low-sodium chicken
   stock

1 cup (235 ml) white vinegar
   or cider vinegar

1 cup (235 ml) water

½ cup (120 ml) good-but-not-great
   olive oil

¼ cup (10 g) chopped fresh sage

4 to 6 cloves garlic, chopped

1   The night before you plan to barbecue, prepare the paste. Combine in a food processor the sage, rosemary, head of garlic, and salt. When chopped very fine, begin drizzling the 1½ cups (355 ml) olive oil through the hole in the top of the processor until all is combined.

2   Massage the paste all over the goat sections. Place the goat in a large plastic bag, such as a trash bag, and refrigerate it overnight.

3   The next day, remove the cabrito from the refrigerator and let it sit in the bag at room temperature for 30 minutes.

4   Prepare the smoker for barbecuing, bringing the temperature to 225°F to 250°F (107°C to 120°C).

5   Prepare the mop by warming the chicken stock, vinegar, water, ½ cup (120 ml) olive oil, sage, and garlic cloves in a medium saucepan. Keep the mixture warm.

6   Transfer the cabrito sections to the smoker, placing them directly on the grate, and plan on about 1 hour or so per pound (455 g) of cooking time for each of the parts. The bonier forelegs will likely be at least a pound (455 g) less than the hindquarters. Turn the cabrito and mop it generously once every 30 minutes, or as recommended for your smoker. Make more mop, if you need, if you think you may run out. The cabrito is done when the meat is tender enough to shred with a fork.

7   Let the cabrito sections sit for about 10 minutes and then slice or pull the meat and serve right away.

Whether you hunt venison or buy it farm raised, it's a good choice for barbecuing. The backstrap is particularly prized for its tenderness. All cuts of the meat take well to smoking, but take care to avoid drying out such a lean protein. Keep it covered tightly and avoid overcooking. You'll be rewarded with a truly special dining experience. I add some Worcestershire powder to the dry rub here because I always have it on hand. I like the extra nuance of flavor, but don't feel like it's essential since you will be adding a Worcestershire sauce-enhanced butter to the finished dish.

VENISON BACKSTRAP WITH WORCESTERSHIRE BUTTER

PREPARATION TIME: 30 MINUTES

COOKING TIME: ABOUT 30 MINUTES

SERVES 6

VENISON DRY RUB

1½ teaspoons kosher salt or coarse
　　sea salt

1 teaspoon coarsely ground
　　black pepper

½ teaspoon ground dried mild
　　red chile, such as ancho or
　　New Mexican

½ teaspoon Worcestershire powder
　　(optional)

¼ teaspoon ground ginger

1 tablespoon (15 ml) vegetable oil

1 (2½- to 3-pound [1.1- to 1.4-kg]
　　venison backstrap (tenderloin),
　　cut into 6 steaks, each about
　　1-inch (2.5 cm) thick

WORCESTERSHIRE BUTTER

4 tablespoons (55 g) unsalted butter

1 teaspoon Worcestershire sauce

1 Combine the salt, black pepper, chile, Worcestershire powder, and ginger in a small bowl. Sprinkle the mixture over the venison and pat it on all the sides of the steaks. (This will be a lighter coat of rub than I recommend on most other meats.)

2 Prepare the smoker for barbecuing, bringing the temperature to 225°F to 250°F (107°C to 120°C).

3 On your stovetop, in a heavy skillet, warm the vegetable oil over high heat. Add the venison steaks and sear on both sides, very quickly (just a matter of seconds).

4 Transfer the venison immediately to the smoker, placing it directly on the grate. Cook until the meat absorbs the smoke lightly and is medium rare at 135°F to 140°F (57°C to 60°C), about 25 to 35 minutes.

5 While the venison smokes, prepare the Worcestershire Butter. Melt the butter in a small skillet over low heat and stir in the Worcestershire sauce. Keep warm.

6 Serve the venison steaks immediately, topped with spoonfuls of Worcestershire Butter.

One of my favorite things to make with ground venison isn't burgers but sort of a fancier version of a meatloaf—a rich pâté. You need to make it at least a day ahead of when you plan to serve it. The pâté has a fair number of ingredients, but essentially, you just mix them all up together and then let it soak up smoke. Enjoy it with some crusty country bread and a nice Texas red wine.

VENISON PÂTÉ

PREPARATION TIME: 45 MINUTES, PLUS OVERNIGHT REFRIGERATION

COOKING TIME: ABOUT 3 HOURS

SERVES 10 OR MORE

½ cup (40 g) chopped bacon

4 tablespoons (55 g) salted butter

1 cup (160 g) chopped shallots

4 large cloves garlic, minced

1¼ pounds (570 g) ground venison

½ pound (225 g) ground pork butt

½ cup (25 g) fresh bread crumbs
  soaked in ¼ cup (60 ml) milk

¼ cup (60 ml) brandy

2 tablespoons (28 ml) dry red wine

½ cup (65 g) diced dried peaches
  or apricots

½ cup (62 g) whole pistachios, raw

1 large egg

1 tablespoon (15 g) Dijon mustard

1 tablespoon (4 g) minced fresh
  tarragon or 1½ teaspoons
  dried tarragon

1 tablespoon (19 g) kosher salt
  or coarse sea salt

2 teaspoons freshly ground
  black pepper

Dijon mustard, cornichons or other
  pickles, and slices of crusty bread,
  if desired, for serving

1   Prepare your smoker for barbecuing, bringing the temperature to 225°F to 250°F (107°C to 120°C).

2   Fry the bacon in a heavy skillet over medium heat until just crisp. Remove it with a slotted spoon and reserve it on a paper-towel–lined plate. Add the butter to the drippings, melt it, and stir in the shallots and garlic. Cook them slowly, over medium heat, until very soft and pale yellow. Spoon the mixture into a large bowl and add the cooked bacon, venison, pork, soaked bread-crumbs, brandy, wine, peaches, pistachios, egg, mustard, tarragon, salt, and black pepper.

3   Spoon the mixture into a large loaf pan. Pat it down and smooth the surface. Cover the pan loosely with foil. You want it to more or less stew in its own juices starting out.

4   In any smoker other than a bullet smoker (water smoker), place the loaf pan in a large pan of warm water, making sure the water comes 1 to 2 inches (2.5 to 5 cm) up the sides of the loaf pan. Transfer the pans to the smoker. Plan on a total cooking time of 2¾ to 3¼ hours. Cook the pâté for 1 hour and then remove the foil. Continue cooking until it shrinks from the sides of the pan and its internal temperature measured on an instant-read thermometer reads 160°F (71°C).

5   Cool the pâté for about 30 minutes. Wrap the pan in plastic wrap and weight the top of the pâté down with a couple of cans from your pantry. Chill at least overnight or for a full 24 hours.

6   Serve the pâté chilled, in small slices, with mustard, cornichon, and bread, if desired.

You might expect a mighty American bison to have a brisket twice the size of a beef brisket. However, the bison's heft is in its shoulders and back, and the brisket tends towards a petite 3 or 4 pounds (1.4 to 1.8 kg). You may not have a lot of choice on the size of this, so if your brisket is slightly larger or smaller, adjust the cooking time, keeping in mind about 1 hour per pound (455 g). I like bison smoked with at least a little mesquite.

BISON BRISKET

PREPARATION TIME: 15 MINUTES

COOKING TIME: ABOUT 3½ HOURS

SERVES 6

1 tablespoon (11 g) yellow mustard
1 (3½-pound [1.6-kg]) bison brisket
¼ cup (42 g) Dalmatian Rub
   (page 43)
½ batch Beer Mop for Beef and Just
   about Everything (page 47)

1   Coat the brisket with the mustard, rubbing it all over. Massage the brisket with the dry rub. Cover with plastic and let it sit at room temperature while firing up the smoker.

2   Prepare the smoker for barbecuing, bringing the temperature to 225°F to 250°F (107°C to 120°C).

3   Transfer the brisket to the smoker, placing it directly on the grate. Keep the mop warm over low heat. Mop the brisket about every 45 minutes or so. The brisket is done when the internal temperature reaches about 195°F (91°C) and the meat shreds easily.

4   Tent with foil and let sit for 15 minutes. Slice the meat thinly across the grain and serve.

CHAPTER 7

CHICKEN, TURKEY, AND GAME BIRDS

Birds of all sizes, from quail to chickens, ducks, and turkeys, all benefit from real wood smoke. Grilled chicken so often is dried out or scorched, problems that are easily avoided when the temperature is turned down into the Q range. I actually do cook some poultry a little higher than most meats, around 300°F (150°C), so that the skin can develop some crispness but in that temperature range, there's no chance of a burned bird.

Beer-can chicken is still a crowd-pleaser after all these years. My original barbecue mentor, Wayne Whitworth, liked to mount a half dozen of these chickens side by side in the pit and then cross their legs so it looked like a high-stepping chorus line when the smoker was opened. It never fails to crack people up to this day. Does the beer add all that much flavor? Maybe not, but it sure adds to the fun.

BEER-CAN CHICKEN

PREPARATION TIME: 30 MINUTES, PLUS OVERNIGHT REFRIGERATION

COOKING TIME: 3 TO 3½ HOURS

SERVES 5 TO 6

POULTRY RUB

¼ cup (28 g) sweet paprika

2 tablespoons (14 g) smoked paprika

2 tablespoons (24 g) celery salt

2 tablespoons (12 g) finely ground black pepper

1 tablespoon (7 g) onion powder

1½ teaspoons dry mustard

1½ teaspoons sugar

2 (3½-pound [1.6-kg] each) whole chickens, trimmed of any excess neck skin or fat

2 (12-ounce [355-ml] each) cans beer (pick something you like to drink.)

1 The night before you plan to barbecue, prepare the dry rub. Combine the sweet paprika, smoked paprika, celery salt, black pepper, onion powder, dry mustard, and sugar in a small bowl. Set aside 2 tablespoons (20 g) of the rub.

2 Massage the chickens thoroughly with the rub, inside and out, working the mixture as far as possible under the skin without tearing it. Cover the chickens and refrigerate them overnight.

3 The next day, prepare the smoker for barbecuing, bringing the temperature to 275°F to 300°F (140°C to 150°C).

4 Remove the chickens from the refrigerator and let them sit at room temperature for about 30 minutes.

5 While you wait, open the two beer cans and drink or set aside half of each beer. With a can opener, remove the tops of the half-empty cans. Spoon 1 tablespoon (10 g) of the reserved rub into each can. Insert a beer can into the bottom cavity of one chicken, balancing the bird so it stays upright with its legs in front of it bent forward. Repeat with the other beer can and chicken.

6 Transfer each beer-can chicken to the smoker's cooking grate, making sure each is sitting level. Cook for 3 to 3½ hours. When the chickens are done, their legs will move freely and the internal temperature of each should read 180°F to 185°F (82°C to 85°C) on an instant-read thermometer.

7 Carefully, remove each chicken from its beer-can throne. Remove the skin if you wish. Carve the chickens and serve.

Chicken can absorb a lot of spice, as this Tex-Mex chile-fueled rub here proves. After smoking, the chicken can be pulled and used as is or as a filling for tacos, sandwiches, burritos, and more.

PULLED POLLO

PREPARATION TIME: 30 MINUTES

COOKING TIME: ABOUT 3 HOURS

SERVES 5 TO 6

2 (3½-pound [1.6-kg]) chickens, trimmed of any excess neck skin or fat

1 tablespoon (14 g) salted butter, melted

½ cup (80 g) Chile Dust (page 45)

1   The night before you plan to barbecue, massage the chickens first with the melted butter and then with the Chile Dust rub, inside and out, working the mixture as far as possible under the skin without tearing it. Cover the chickens and refrigerate them overnight.

2   The next day, prepare the smoker for barbecuing, bringing the temperature to 275°F to 300°F (140°C to 150°C).

3   Remove the chickens from the refrigerator and let them sit at room temperature for about 30 minutes.

4   Transfer the chickens to the smoker, laying them on the grate breast-side down. Cook for about 3 hours, turning each chicken breast-side up about halfway through the cooking time. When the chickens are done, their legs will move freely and the internal temperature of each should read 180°F to 185°F (82°C to 85°C) on an instant-read thermometer.

5   Remove the skins and when cool enough to handle, pull the chicken from the bones. Using Bear Paws (page 37), your fingers, or two forks, shred the chicken into bite-size pieces and serve.

Texas cookbooks are filled with dishes flavored with Waco-born Dr Pepper. You'll even find a Dr Pepper–based recipe in this book (page 70). Here's another dish, something a little more unexpected perhaps, incorporating a soft drink. My Austin-based stepdaughter has a number of Filipino colleagues who love this variation on barbecued chicken.

SPRITE-LY FILIPINO CHICKEN

PREPARATION TIME: 30 MINUTES, PLUS 1 HOUR'S REFRIGERATION

COOKING TIME: 1 TO 1¼ HOURS

SERVES 6

SPRITE-LY MARINADE

1 cup (235 ml) cider or white vinegar

½ cup (120 ml) soy sauce

½ cup (120 g) ketchup

½ cup (115 g) packed light
   or dark brown sugar

1 tablespoon (6 g) cracked
   black pepper

4 bay leaves

4 large cloves garlic

1 teaspoon kosher salt or coarse
   sea salt

12 ounces (355 ml) Sprite, 7Up,
   or other lemon-lime soda

12 bone-in, skin-on chicken thighs

Juice of 1 large lime

1   In a blender, combine the vinegar, soy sauce, ketchup, brown sugar, black pepper, bay leaves, garlic, and salt. Blitz until the peppercorns and bay leaves are finely ground. Pour the soda into the blender and stir.

2   Loosen the skin on the chicken thighs as much as you can without tearing the skin. Place the thighs in a shallow baking dish that can hold them pretty much in a single layer. Pour the marinade over the top. With your fingers, rub some of the marinade under the skin of each thigh. Turn the chicken as needed to coat evenly. Cover the dish and refrigerate for 1 hour.

3   Prepare the smoker for barbecuing, bringing the temperature to 275°F to 300°F (140°C to 150°C).

4   Remove the chicken from the refrigerator and drain the marinade into a small saucepan. Let the chicken sit uncovered. Bring the marinade to a rolling boil and reduce it by about half to use as a sauce. Remove it from the heat, stir in the lime juice, and reserve.

5   Transfer the chicken to the smoker, placing it directly on the grate, and cook for about 1 hour until the chicken is very tender and the juices run clear when a skewer is inserted into a thigh.

6   Serve the chicken right away, accompanied by the reduced sauce.

Lots of folks refer to grilled chicken as barbecued chicken. We know better, don't we? Here's an easy-to-smoke, easy-to-eat version of truly barbecued chicken. You can replace the breast with boneless thighs if you prefer. In either case, it's pretty fast cooking. If you don't have easy access to tamarind paste, skip it and add a couple of teaspoons of lime juice in its place. The flavor will be a bit different, but the juice will add some of the desired tang to the sauce.

BACKYARD BBQ'D CHICKEN BREASTS

PREPARATION TIME: 30 MINUTES

COOKING TIME: 30 TO 45 MINUTES

SERVES 6

CHICKEN BBQ SAUCE

½ cup (120 ml) orange juice

¼ cup plus 2 tablespoons (88 ml) chicken stock

¼ cup plus 1 tablespoon (75 g) chipotle ketchup or barbecue sauce, or the same amount of regular ketchup or barbecue sauce mixed with 1 to 2 minced canned chipotle chiles

¼ cup (80 g) orange marmalade

1 tablespoon (16 g) tamarind paste (concentrate)

1 tablespoon (14 g) salted butter

1 tablespoon (15 ml) garlic-flavored oil or vegetable oil

1 teaspoon kosher salt or coarse sea salt

6 medium boneless, skinless chicken breasts, pounded lightly to an even thickness

1 Prepare the sauce. Stir together the orange juice, chicken stock, chipotle ketchup, marmalade, tamarind paste, and butter in a small saucepan and bring to a boil over medium heat. Reduce the heat to maintain a bare simmer and cook for about 5 minutes. (The sauce can be made a day or two ahead, if you prefer.)

2 Prepare the smoker for barbecuing, bringing the temperature to 200°F to 225°F (93°C to 107°C).

3 Combine the oil and salt in a small bowl and rub it over the chicken breasts. Transfer the chicken to the smoker, placing it directly on the grate. Cook for a total of about 30 minutes until cooked through. Brush the tops of the chicken breasts with about ½ cup (120 ml) of the sauce. Continue cooking about 10 minutes more until the sauce is a little tacky.

4 Serve the chicken immediately with more sauce on the side.

SIX MORE THINGS TO DO WITH SMOKED CHICKEN

Chicken and Chihuahua Cheese Rellenos.
For four stuffed chiles, roast 4 plump poblano chiles over a gas stove burner or under the broiler briefly until blackened and blistered. Pull off the peel. Cut a slit from end to end on one side of each chile. At the stem end of each pod, cut across the top of the slit about 1 inch (2.5 cm), so that you have a T-shape cut. Stuff the chiles with a mixture of ¾ cup (105 g) shredded barbecued chicken and 1½ cups (173 g) shredded Chihuahua cheese (substitute Monterey Jack if you prefer). Place the stuffed chiles on a baking sheet and bake in a 350°F (180°C, or gas mark 4) oven until heated through, about 15 minutes. Serve with salsa or chile sauce, if you like.

Open-Faced Chicken Enchiladas. For four servings, warm 1 cup (235 ml) chile verde sauce or salsa in a saucepan. Dunk eight, 6-inch (15 cm) corn tortillas into the sauce. Place the tortillas side by side on an oiled baking sheet. Top each with about ⅓ cup (47 g) shredded smoked chicken. Top each with about ⅓ cup (38 g) shredded mild Cheddar or Monterey Jack cheese. Bake at 375°F (190°C, or gas mark 5) until the chicken is warmed through and cheese is melted and bubbly, about 8 minutes. Top with pico de gallo (chopped tomatoes, jalapeños, and onions) and serve.

Pulled Chicken Sandwiches. Use your imagination on these. I like to start with a toasted potato roll or white bread bun or even Texas toast. Top with coleslaw or even kimchi or maybe a pile of dill pickles, just something that can contribute a nice tang to the sandwich. Plan on at least ½ cup (70 g) shredded chicken per sandwich.

Chicken Spring Rolls. Make a dipping sauce, combining 3 tablespoons of Asian fish sauce (45 ml), 3 tablespoons (39 g) sugar, the juice of 1 lime, and about ⅓ cup (80 ml) water. Add about 1 teaspoon very thinly sliced red or green Thai or serrano chiles. Soak rice paper spring roll wrappers one at a time. Drain the wrapper, and on each one, sprinkle a couple of tablespoons of smoked chicken, some soaked cellophane noodles, and bits of carrot or cucumber and chopped basil, mint, or cilantro, or a combination, to taste. Form the wrapper into a firm tube, first turning in the sides and then folding the bottom up over the filling and rolling it all up. Repeat with remaining wrappers and filling ingredients. Slice in half on the diagonal and serve with the sauce.

Chicken Lettuce Wraps. Make the dipping sauce for the spring rolls above. Pile warm shredded chicken in butter lettuce leaves and add a few bits of cucumber or carrot and maybe a leaf or two of mint or basil. Dip in sauce and devour.

Smoked Chicken Salad. Mix whatever quantity of chicken you have with enough mayonnaise to moisten it thoroughly. Mix in chopped celery, pecans, and halved green or red seedless grapes to taste. I like a few poppy seeds added for a little crunch too. Chill for about 30 minutes for flavors to mingle before serving.

In Texas history classes, kids learn that Spanish explorers celebrated a feast of Thanksgiving near present-day El Paso long before the Pilgrims left England. Plenty of Americans elsewhere have no idea. I don't think it needs to be Thanksgiving to smoke up a turkey breast, a much easier task than a whole turkey. If I do want a whole smoked turkey, I order one from Greenberg's (page 117).

BARBECUED PEPPERED TURKEY BREAST

PREPARATION TIME: 30 MINUTES, PLUS OVERNIGHT REFRIGERATION

COOKING TIME: 6 TO 7 HOURS

SERVES 6 TO 8

INJECTION LIQUID

6 tablespoons (85 g) salted butter, melted

2 tablespoons (28 ml) vegetable oil

2 tablespoons (28 ml) chicken stock

1 to 2 teaspoons Worcestershire sauce

1 (5- to 6-pound [2.3- to 2.7-kg]) boneless turkey breast, preferably skin on

½ cup (83 g) Dalmatian Rub (page 43)

1 The night before you plan to barbecue, mix the butter, oil, chicken stock, and Worcestershire sauce together in a small bowl. With a kitchen syringe, inject the liquid deep into the turkey breast in a half-dozen places. (See sidebar for details.)

2 Massage the breast well with the Dalmatian Rub, rubbing it over and under the skin. Place the breast in a plastic bag and refrigerate it overnight.

3 Prepare the smoker for barbecuing, bringing the temperature to 225°F to 250°F (107°C to 120°C). Let the turkey breast sit in the bag at room temperature while the smoker heats.

4 Transfer the turkey breast to the smoker, placing it skin-side up directly on the grate. Cook for 1 to 1¼ hours per pound (455 g) until the internal temperature reaches 160°F (71°C).

5 Let sit for 15 minutes before carving and serving.

To Inject Your Bird

For a whole chicken or turkey breast, it's not uncommon to use an injection liquid. I melt together 6 tablespoons (85 g) salted butter with a couple tablespoons (120 ml) each of vegetable oil and flavorful chicken stock and a teaspoon or two of Worcestershire sauce. Draw the liquid into an injector and then poke it deep into the meat and slowly inject the liquid. Don't rush it or the liquid will come squirting back at you. Once you have injected one spot, use the same hole in the surface to inject the meat in several different directions. Then, move a few inches (10 cm) and repeat the process until you have fairly good coverage of the meat. Some of the butter will harden, but persevere. The mixture is more than you need for a single chicken, but you have to have a certain quantity to draw the liquid up into the injector.

In spite of—or perhaps because of—all the over-the-top fried food (fried butter, anyone?) at the State Fair of Texas each fall, I gravitate toward the smoked turkey legs instead. Maybe it's because of the powerful feeling of carrying around something just slightly smaller than baseball bat. More likely, it's just that if you present me with the option of fried food versus barbecue, Q will win every time. Here's a well-seasoned version of that other fair favorite.

JERK-Y TURKEY LEGS

PREPARATION TIME: 30 MINUTES,
PLUS OVERNIGHT REFRIGERATION

COOKING TIME: 3 TO 3½ HOURS

SERVES 8

8 turkey drumsticks

JERK PASTE

8 green onions, cut into several
   chunks each

3 large cloves garlic

1 Scotch bonnet or habanero chile

Juice of 1 large lime

2 tablespoons (28 ml) vegetable oil

2 tablespoons (12 g) ground allspice

1 tablespoon (15 g) packed light
   or dark brown sugar

2 teaspoons dried thyme

2 teaspoons dried ginger

2 teaspoons ground cinnamon

2 teaspoons kosher salt or coarse
   sea salt

2 teaspoons finely ground
   black pepper

1 teaspoon ground nutmeg

1 At least 4 hours and up to the night before you plan to barbecue, loosen the skin on the turkey legs by running your fingers under it as far as possible without tearing the skin.

2 In a blender, combine the green onion, garlic, chile, lime juice, oil, allspice, brown sugar, thyme, ginger, cinnamon, salt, black pepper, and nutmeg. Blend until smooth. If the mixture doesn't blend easily, add a teaspoon or two of water to help it along.

3 Massage the drumsticks well with the paste, rubbing it over and under the skin, working it as far under the skin as possible without tearing it. Place the drumsticks in a plastic bag and refrigerate overnight.

4 Prepare the smoker for barbecuing, bringing the temperature to 225°F to 250°F (107°C to 120°C).

5 Remove the turkey legs from the refrigerator and let them sit uncovered at room temperature for about 30 minutes.

6 Transfer the drumsticks to the smoker, placing them directly on the grate. Cook until the leg juices run clear, 3 to 3½ hours. The internal temperature should be 170°F (77°C), if you can get a good reading without hitting bone.

7 Serve the legs hot, to be eaten with your fingers.

Turkey Talk

Once I mastered smoking turkey for the sake of knowing I could do it myself, I decided I didn't often need to do it. Now I love smoked turkey, but I don't make it that often because of Sam Greenberg. The Jewish Greenberg clan of Tyler fell into the business of hickory-smoking turkeys three generations ago, and Sam runs one of the state's most loved businesses today. Despite substantial growth, everything about the process is done by hand except for the final stapling of boxes in which the turkeys are shipped. My first Greenberg's turkey was a gift back in the mid-1980s. When I opened the carton, I was nearly knocked over by the richness of the hickory scent, the scent of real barbecue. I've been enjoying the magnificent mahogany-skinned birds ever since. Order online from gobblegobble.com.

Texas tea refers to oil, and not the kind used in cooking. However, it makes a dandy title for this vaguely Asian tea-smoked whole duck. This is a project, and it involves steaming and smoking, but it's easier to master than barbecued brisket. To completely blow away your friends, add a simple but impressive citrus-scented ponzu sauce.

TEXAS TEA-SMOKED DUCK

PREPARATION TIME: 2 HOURS, PLUS AT LEAST 8 HOURS' REFRIGERATION

COOKING TIME: 1½ HOURS STEAMING, 4 TO 4½ HOURS SMOKING

SERVES 4 TO 6

DUCK PASTE

2 medium oranges

¼ cup (24 g) minced fresh ginger

1½ tablespoons (28 g) kosher salt or coarse sea salt

1 tablespoon (7 g) ground cinnamon

1 teaspoon Chinese five-spice powder

2 (4- to 4½-pound [1.8- to 2-kg]) ducks

5 tablespoons (10 g) loose black tea leaves

12 cups (2.8 L) water

3 whole cinnamon sticks

1 tablespoon (5 g) Szechuan peppercorns

2 whole star anise

PONZU SAUCE

2 tablespoons (28 ml) hot water

1 teaspoon sugar

1 tablespoon (15 ml) mirin (sweet Japanese rice wine)

1 tablespoon (15 ml) rice vinegar

1 tablespoon (15 ml) soy sauce

1 tablespoon (15 ml) orange juice

1 tablespoon (15 ml) fresh lime juice

4 green onions

1 At least 10 to 24 hours before you plan to barbecue, make the paste in a bowl by using the zest of an orange, the juice of two oranges, ginger, cinnamon, five-spice, and salt. Rub the ducks with the paste thoroughly inside and out, and over and under the skin, being careful to avoid tearing the skin. Wrap the ducks and refrigerate them for at least 8 hours.

2 About 2 hours before you plan to barbecue, take the ducks from the refrigerator and let them sit uncovered for 30 minutes.

3 Prepare the tea for steaming the ducks. Place the tea leaves in a large heatproof bowl. Bring the water just to a boil and pour it over the tea leaves. Let the mixture steep for 10 minutes. Pour the tea through a strainer into a large saucepan. Place the leftover tea leaves in a disposable pie pan or other smokeproof dish and add reserved orange peel in several pieces, cinnamon sticks, peppercorns, and star anise. Set aside.

4 Arrange a large bamboo steamer over the saucepan of tea and place the ducks in the steamer. (If one steamer isn't large enough for the two ducks, make a double batch of tea and use two saucepans and steamers.) Steam the ducks over medium-high heat for 1½ hours. Discard the greasy steaming liquid.

5 Prepare your smoker for barbecuing, bringing the temperature to 200°F to 250°F (93°C to 120°C).

6 Place the pan of tea leaves and spices on your smoker's lower grate or shelf. If it doesn't have such a thing, place the pan on the cooking grate as close to the heat source as possible. Transfer the ducks to the smoker, placing them breast-side up on the grate. Cook for 4 to 4½ hours. The ducks will have already been cooked through from the steaming, so you don't need to check the temperature of the meat. You want the skin to darken to a deep mahogany and for the ducks' leg joints to move freely.

7 While the ducks are smoking, make the Ponzu Sauce. Stir together the hot water with the sugar in a small bowl until sugar dissolves. Stir in the mirin, rice vinegar, soy sauce, 1 tablespoon orange juice, and lime juice and reserve at room temperature.

8 Slice the ducks or place them whole on a platter and tear apart with chopsticks. Scatter with green onions. Serve with the Ponzu Sauce.

Here's a simpler duck preparation that will still earn you kudos. There's a nice kick of spice with this.

DUCK BREAST WITH BARBECUE VINAIGRETTE

PREPARATION TIME: 5 MINUTES

COOKING TIME: 20 MINUTES STEAMING, 60 TO 75 MINUTES SMOKING

SERVES 6

6 (5-ounce [140-g]) skin-on
   duck breasts
3 tablespoons (30 g) Red Dirt
   (page 44)
1 batch Citrus Barbecue Vinaigrette
   (page 148)

1 Arrange a large bamboo steamer over a saucepan of water and place the duck breasts in the steamer, skin-side down. Steam over medium-high heat for 20 minutes. Discard the greasy steaming liquid.

2 Massage the duck breasts with the Red Dirt rub, over and under the skin.

3 Prepare your smoker for barbecuing by bringing the temperature to 200°F to 250°F (93°C to 120°C).

4 Transfer the duck breasts to the smoker, placing them skin-side up directly on the grate, and cook for 60 to 75 minutes. The breasts should be done but still juicy, with some caramelized edges.

5 Let the duck breasts sit for 5 minutes before slicing on the diagonal. Serve with vinaigrette pooled under or spooned over the breasts.

These diminutive birds are a Texas classic, whether hunted or farm raised.

HONEY-GLAZED CHORIZO-STUFFED QUAIL

PREPARATION TIME: 30 MINUTES

COOKING TIME: ABOUT 1½ HOURS

SERVES 6

6 ounces (170 g) bulk chorizo
    sausage

6 cloves garlic, sliced

6 semi-boned quail

1 tablespoon (15 ml) extra-virgin
    olive oil

1 teaspoon kosher salt or coarse
    sea salt

2 tablespoons (40 ml) honey

1. Prepare the smoker for barbecuing, bringing the temperature to 200°F to 220°F (93°C to 104°C).

2. In a small skillet on the stovetop, fry the chorizo over medium heat until cooked through, about 5 minutes. Add the garlic and cook for another minute. Pour off any excess fat.

3. Prepare the quail, cutting off their necks if necessary. Rub the quail with the olive oil inside and out, and then sprinkle them evenly with salt. Stuff each quail with a portion of the chorizo. Truss the tiny legs, if you like.

4. Transfer the quail to the smoker, placing them on the grate breast-side down. Cook the quail 1¼ hours. Turn the quail breast sides up and brush with honey. Continue smoking for 15 to 30 more minutes until the quail are well browned and their legs move easily at the joints. Serve immediately.

"We are living, deliciously and indisputably, in the golden age of BBQ."

TEXAS MONTHLY, JUNE 2017

CHAPTER 8

GULF SEAFOOD AND LAKE FISH

Long before brisket, fish was the favorite barbecued fare in the Americas. When Spanish explorers arrived centuries ago, Amerindians were smoking fish over wood fires in the technique that the Spanish called *barbacoa*. Lots of commercially available smoked fish and seafood is cold-smoked or cured rather than smoked in a barbecue manner, which is how its cooked in these recipes. With 367 miles (591 km) of Gulf coastline and 188 lakes, Texas has no shortage of fish and seafood to put in the barbecue pit.

Support your local fishermen and women. I would far prefer to look for and purchase Gulf shrimp when available than get seafood shipped from the other side of the world. This recipe mimics the flavors in a shrimp boil while adding another dimension to the dish.

GULF OF GALVESTON SHRIMP "SMOKE" WITH CORN AND SAUSAGE

PREPARATION TIME: 30 MINUTES

COOKING TIME: ABOUT 20 MINUTES

SERVES 8

2 pounds (900 g) peeled large
   tail-on shrimp
2 tablespoons (28 ml) vegetable oil,
   divided
2 tablespoons (20 g) Wild Willy's
   Number One-derful Rub (page 43),
   divided
4 ears corn, halved
8 cooked spicy sausage links, 4 to
   5 ounces (115 to 140 g) each
2 tablespoons (28 g) unsalted butter,
   melted

1 Prepare the smoker for barbecuing, bringing the temperature to 200°F to 220°F (93°C to 104°C).

2 Place the shrimp in a bowl and toss with 1 tablespoon (15 ml) of the oil and 1 tablespoon (10 g) of dry rub. Place the corn in another large bowl and rub it with the remaining oil, then massage in the remaining dry rub.

3 Arrange the shrimp on a grill rack more or less in a single layer. If the rack is large enough, add the corn and sausage to it too. Otherwise, simply place the corn and sausage directly in the smoker.

4 Cook the shrimp and sausage for about 20 minutes until the shrimp are opaque and lightly pink. Since the sausage is cooked, it will be ready at the same time. Depending on the freshness and type of corn, it may be ready too or may require a few more minutes in the smoker.

5 Pile the corn and sausage around the sides of a platter and place the shrimp in the center. Drizzle with the melted butter and serve right away.

Vietnamese flavors have added vibrancy to the Texas food culture and within a generation have woven completely into the fabric of the state. Here's an example that adds smoke to a fairly classic dish. You'll need to smoke the shrimp as in the Vietnamese Shrimp recipe on page 58, so that's what's referred to by the cooking time listed here.

VIETNAMESE LEMONGRASS SHRIMP AND NOODLES

PREPARATION TIME: 45 MINUTES

COOKING TIME: ABOUT 20 MINUTES

SERVES 4

About 8 ounces (225 g) dried rice
   vermicelli noodles (*bún*)

Hot water

LEMONGRASS DRESSING

½ cup (120 ml) rice vinegar

¼ cup (50 g) sugar

2 tablespoons (28 ml) Asian fish
   sauce

2 tablespoons (10 g) chopped
   lemongrass (use the tender inner
   portion of the stalk)

1 teaspoon chopped fresh ginger

1 teaspoon Asian chile paste
   or sauce

1 batch Vietnamese Shrimp (page
   58), warm or chilled for up to
   1 day

1 cup (119 g) cucumber matchsticks

½ cup (61 g) carrot matchsticks

1   Place the vermicelli in a medium bowl and cover with hot water. Soak about 15 minutes until the noodles are pliable but still a bit al dente.

2   While the noodles soak, prepare the Lemongrass Dressing. Combine the rice vinegar, fish sauce, lemongrass, ginger, and chile paste in a blender and puree.

3   When the noodles are ready, drain them and toss them with the Lemongrass Dressing.

4   Divide the noodles among four large shallow bowls. Scatter the cucumbers and carrots equally over the noodles and then arrange the shrimp equally over the top. Serve.

I associate crawfish with the southeast part of Texas and Cajun country, though my late husband recalled with great fondness hunting for them around his grandparents' home in Sprinkle, just outside of Austin. Add smoke to them before turning them into a rich chowder, which is enhanced further by their pairing with zesty andouille sausage. If it's difficult to find crawfish, cooked peeled medium shrimp can be substituted. Since both the crawfish and sausage are already cooked, it's just a matter of giving them smoky flavor before putting them in the chowder. You can skip the bread bowls if you like, but they're sure a nice touch.

CRAWDAD-ANDOUILLE CHOWDER

PREPARATION TIME: 45 MINUTES

COOKING TIME: ABOUT 10 MINUTES SMOKING, 20 MINUTES ON THE STOVETOP

SERVES 6

1 pound (455 g) peeled cooked
    crawfish tails
1 tablespoon (15 ml) vegetable oil
1 teaspoon Tabasco or other
    hot sauce
4 to 6 ounces (115 to 170 g) cooked
    andouille sausage, sliced thin

CHOWDER
2 tablespoons (28 ml) vegetable oil
2 tablespoons (16 g)
    all-purpose flour
1 medium onion, diced fine
1 small red bell pepper, diced fine
1 celery stalk, chopped fine
2 medium carrots, chopped
1 small baking potato, about 8
    ounces (225 g), peeled and diced
1 teaspoon dried thyme
1 bay leaf
3 cups (700 ml) low-sodium
    chicken stock
12 ounces (355 ml) seafood stock
    or bottled clam juice
1 cup (235 ml) half-and-half
Bread bowls, for serving

1   Prepare your smoker for barbecuing, bringing the temperature to 225°F to 250°F (107°C to 120°C).

2   Toss the crawfish together in a bowl with 1 tablespoon (15 ml) oil and Tabasco sauce. Arrange the crawfish and the andouille slices on a small mesh grill rack or piece of heavy-duty foil that will hold everything in one layer. Transfer the crawfish and andouille to the smoker as far from the heat as possible and smoke for 10 to 12 minutes. Reserve.

3   Prepare the chowder, working on either a side burner or in your kitchen. Warm the 2 tablespoons (28 ml) oil in a heavy stockpot or deep skillet over medium-high heat. Sprinkle the flour evenly over the oil. Stir the mixture constantly until it turns a light nutty brown. Immediately stir in the onion, red bell pepper, celery, carrots, and potato and turn the heat down to medium low. Stir in the thyme and bay leaf. Cook until the vegetables begin to soften, about 10 minutes.

4   Pour in the chicken and seafood stock and continue cooking about 20 minutes more, until the vegetables are tender. Pour in the half-and-half. Add the crawfish-andouille mixture and any juices and heat through. Spoon into bread bowls and serve.

The Texas portion of the Gulf of Mexico has huge numbers of oyster beds. Lightly smoke some of those bivalves and then paint them with a lively chile-and-lime-enhanced butter. Serve with margaritas or palomas. There's nothing better.

OYSTERS WITH CHIPOTLE BUTTER

PREPARATION TIME: 15 MINUTES

COOKING TIME:30 MINUTES

MAKES 2 DOZEN

CHIPOTLE BUTTER

8 tablespoons (112 g) unsalted
    butter

1 canned chipotle chile, minced,
    plus 1 teaspoon adobo sauce
    from the can

2 teaspoons fresh lime juice

2 dozen oysters, shucked, bottom
    shells and liquor (juices) reserved

2 dozen ice cubes

1   Prepare the smoker for barbecuing, bringing the temperature to 180°F to 200°F (82°C to 93°C).

2   Melt the butter over low heat and stir in the chipotle chile and lime juice. Keep warm.

3   Place the ice cubes in a shallow smokeproof baking dish. Place the oysters on the half-shell on a small grill rack and place the rack over the ice-filled pan.

4   Place the oysters and the ice pan in the smoker as far as possible from the heat source. Cook for about 30 minutes until the oysters are plump and slightly firm but still juicy.

5   Brush them with the Chipotle Butter. Serve with any remaining butter. Slurp up!

A whole fish always make an impression, and barbecuing one is easy since there's no need to turn or otherwise mess with it once it goes into the smoker.

WHOLE STUFFED SNAPPER

PREPARATION TIME: 1 HOUR

COOKING TIME: ABOUT 1 HOUR

SERVES 4 TO 6

1 (3- to 3½-pound [1.4- to 2.3-kg])
  gutted whole red snapper,
  sea bass, or other mild-flavored
  white fish
1 tablespoon (15 ml) extra-virgin
  olive oil
Juice of 2 lemons, divided
1 teaspoon kosher salt or coarse
  sea salt

STUFFING

½ cup (60 g) dry bread crumbs
½ medium onion, chopped
3 tablespoons (12 g) minced
  flat-leaf parsley
2 tablespoons (5 g) minced fresh
  thyme, plus a few fresh thyme
  sprigs for garnish
1 teaspoon Cholula hot sauce
  or other hot sauce

1   Prepare the smoker for barbecuing, bringing the temperature to 180°F to 200°F (82°C to 93°C).

2   Cut three deep diagonal slashes into both sides of the snapper to help it cook evenly and absorb maximum flavor. Rub the fish inside and out with the olive oil and half of the lemon juice, reserving the remaining lemon juice for the stuffing. Sprinkle with the salt.

3   Prepare the stuffing. In a medium bowl, mix together the bread crumbs, onion, parsley, thyme, hot sauce, and reserved lemon juice. Stuff the fish loosely. Place the fish on a greased grill rack.

4   Transfer the snapper to the smoker, as far from the fire as possible. Cook until opaque and flaky, about 20 minutes per pound (455 g). Use a large spatula to move the fish from the grill rack to a large serving platter.

5   Garnish with thyme sprigs. To serve, remove the skin and cut through the fish, watching for its bones. Serve each portion with some of the stuffing.

I love snapper and smoke. Fillets cook almost in an instant, so I find I can satisfy a craving very quickly. The vinaigrette gives the hit of acid that balances the richness of smoke so well.

SNAPPER FILLETS WITH CILANTRO VINAIGRETTE

PREPARATION TIME: 20 MINUTES

COOKING TIME: ABOUT 30 MINUTES

SERVES 4

CILANTRO VINAIGRETTE

1 large shallot, minced

Zest of 1 lemon

3 tablespoons (45 ml) fresh
   lemon juice

1 teaspoon Dijon mustard

½ teaspoon kosher salt or coarse
   sea salt, plus more to taste

½ cup (120 ml) extra-virgin olive oil

1 to 2 tablespoons (1 to 2 g)
   minced cilantro

4 (8-ounce [225-g]) snapper fillets, or
   other mild-flavored white fish fillets

2 tablespoons (28 ml) extra-virgin
   olive oil

1 teaspoon kosher salt or coarse
   sea salt

1 large lemon, thinly sliced

1   Prepare the smoker for barbecuing, bringing the temperature to 180°F to 200°F (82°C to 93°C).

2   Prepare the Cilantro Vinaigrette. Combine the shallot, lemon zest, and lemon juice in
a bowl. Let the mixture sit for about 10 minutes. Whisk in the mustard and ½ teaspoon salt. When combined, whisk in the ½ cup oil, followed by the cilantro. Taste to see if more salt is needed.

3   Brush the flesh side of the fish fillets with 2 tablespoons (28 ml) olive oil and then sprinkle each with a portion of the 1 teaspoon salt. Cover the fillets generously with the lemon slices.

4   Arrange the fish fillets on an oiled small grill rack, skin side down, then transfer the rack to the smoker, placing them directly on the grate as far from the fire as possible. Cook for 25 to 30 minutes until opaque and flaky. Serve right away.

From wade fishing to boat fishing, the Gulf community of Port O'Connor is considered prime turf for harvesting many species of fish. Redfish were considered endangered at one time but have bounced back through good management. "On the half-shell" is the local wags' way of referring to the scales-on skin of fish fillets. Ask your fishmonger to leave the scales on when filleting the fish.

PORT O'CONNOR REDFISH ON THE HALF SHELL

PREPARATION TIME: 15 MINUTES

COOKING TIME: 45 MINUTES

SERVES 4

4 (10-ounce [280-g]) boneless redfish
  or snapper fillets, skin and scales
  left on
2 tablespoons (28 ml) extra-virgin
  olive oil
1 teaspoon kosher salt or coarse
  sea salt
1 teaspoon crushed red pepper flakes
2 medium lemons, sliced very thin

1   Prepare the smoker for barbecuing, bringing the temperature to 180°F to 200°F (82°C to 93°C).

2   Brush the flesh side of the fish fillets with the olive oil, and then sprinkle each with a portion of the salt and red pepper flakes. Cover the fillets generously with the lemon slices.

3   Transfer fish fillets to the smoker, placing them directly on the grate as far from the fire as possible, skin-side down. Cook for about 45 minutes until opaque and flaky. Serve right away.

Steaks from deep-sea tuna are nearly as meaty as beef steaks. Their flavor is so full that a simple pepper-and-salt rub enhances their mild brininess without masking it. The steaks get a quick sear at the end to give them a light crust. Just be careful to avoid overcooking them.

TUNA STEAKS

PREPARATION TIME: 5 MINUTES

COOKING TIME: 20 MINUTES, PLUS A QUICK SEAR ON THE STOVETOP

SERVES 4

4 ahi tuna steaks, about 1 inch (2.5 cm) thick

2 tablespoons (20 g) Dalmatian Rub (page 43)

2 teaspoons vegetable oil

1 large lemon, sliced into 4 wedges

1 Prepare the smoker for barbecuing, bringing the temperature to 180°F to 200°F (82°C to 93°C).

2 Massage the tuna steaks with the rub on both sides.

3 Transfer the tuna steaks to the smoker, placing them directly on the grate. Cook until just barely medium rare, about 20 minutes.

4 On the stovetop, warm a large skillet over high heat. Swirl in the oil, just enough to coat the surface. Sear the tuna steaks quickly on one side only.

5 Serve immediately, seared-side up, accompanied by the lemon wedges.

Fish tacos, however delicious, have become ubiquitous in recent years. These tostadas delight in similar fashion but have an element of surprise. Don't feel you need to make up the Red Dirt dry rub when the recipe only needs 2 teaspoons of the mixture. If you don't have it on hand already, just use a similar amount of a Mexican hot sauce, such as Cholula.

TUNA TOSTADAS WITH TANGY ORANGE MAYONNAISE

PREPARATION TIME: 30 MINUTES

COOKING TIME: 20 MINUTES

SERVES 4

4 (8-ounce [225-g] each) ahi tuna
   steaks, about ½ inch (1 cm) thick
1 tablespoon (15 ml) extra-virgin
   olive oil
2 teaspoons Red Dirt, or Mexican
   hot sauce such as Cholula

TANGY ORANGE MAYONNAISE
½ cup (115 g) mayonnaise
2 tablespoons (28 ml) orange juice
1 teaspoon fresh lime juice
Pinch of Red Dirt or a dash of
   Mexican hot sauce such as Cholula
Juice of 1 lime
2 green onions (green and white
   portions), minced
2 tablespoons (2 g) chopped cilantro
8 crisp corn tostada shells
1 to 2 ripe avocados, diced

1. Prepare the smoker for barbecuing, bringing the temperature to 180°F to 200°F (82°C to 93°C).

2. Rub the tuna steaks with olive oil, then sprinkle with the Red Dirt rub. Cover and let sit at room temperature for about 30 minutes.

3. Prepare the Tangy Orange Mayonnaise, mixing together the mayonnaise, orange juice, 1 teaspoon lime juices, and dry rub. Refrigerate until needed.

4. Transfer the tuna steaks to the smoker, placing them directly on the grate as far from the fire as possible. Cook until the fish is just barely cooked through with a hint of pink still at the center of each steak, about 20 minutes.

5. Cut the tuna into neat ½-inch (1.3 m) cubes and toss with lime juice, green onions, and cilantro. Spoon the tuna mixture equally onto the tostada shells. Top with avocado. Spoon about 1 tablespoon (14 g) of the Tangy Orange Mayonnaise over each tostada. Accompany with the remaining mayonnaise.

Crappie is a freshwater fish from the lakes of Texas. It takes to Cajun seasoning like, well, a fish to water. Substitute another mild-flavored flaky white fish for crappie if it's not available to you.

CAJUN-SEASONED CRAPPIE

PREPARATION TIME: 5 MINUTES

COOKING TIME: ABOUT 20 MINUTES

SERVES 4

4 (6-ounce [170-g] each) crappie
   fillets
   or other white fish fillets
2 tablespoons (28 g) unsalted butter,
   melted
2 tablespoons (18 g) store-bought
   Cajun seasoning

1   Prepare the smoker for barbecuing, bringing the temperature to 180°F to 200°F (82°C to 93°C).

2   Brush the fish fillets with the melted butter and then sprinkle with Cajun seasoning.

3   Arrange the fish fillets on a small oiled grill rack, then transfer the rack to the smoker as far from the fire as possible. Cook until the fish is opaque and flaky, about 20 minutes. Serve right away.

Catfish doesn't have to be fried to be fabulous. This version takes inspiration from Thai and other Asian catfish preparations.

SAUCY LIME AND SWEET CHILE CATFISH

PREPARATION TIME: 5 MINUTES

COOKING TIME: 1 TO 1¼ HOURS

SERVES 6

2 tablespoons (20 g) Dalmatian Rub

½ teaspoon finely ground white
pepper

1 tablespoon (15 ml) vegetable oil

6 (8-ounce [225-g] each) catfish
fillets

½ cup (120 ml) store-bought sweet
Thai chile sauce

Juice of 1 medium lime

1   Prepare the smoker for barbecuing, bringing the temperature to 180°F to 200°F (82°C to 93°C).

2   In a small bowl, stir together the Dalmatian Rub and the white pepper.

3   Brush the catfish fillets with the oil and sprinkle with the dry rub.

4   Transfer the catfish to the smoker, placing it directly on the grate as far from the fire as possible. Cook the fillets for 1 to 1¼ hours until opaque and firm but still flaky.

5   Mix together the sweet Thai chile sauce and lime juice. Serve the fillets immediately, topped with big spoonfuls of the sauce.

FROM THE
GREAT INDOORS

CHAPTER 9

SAUCES AND CONDIMENTS

I think by now we've agreed that Texas Q and sauce can peacefully coexist and actually create some pretty great pairings. But don't stop with the classics. You can top your barbecue with just about anything you wish, such as a spicy salty snack; my favorite is crumbled Crunchy Flamin' Hot Limón Cheetos.

"Barbecue sauce is like a beautiful woman. If it's too sweet, it's bound to be hiding something."

—LYLE LOVETT

Try this sauce on spare ribs, back ribs, and certainly on chopped beef sandwiches.

EAST TEXAS MOLASSES BBQ SAUCE

PREPARATION TIME: 15 MINUTES

COOKING TIME: 20 MINUTES

MAKES APPROXIMATELY 2 CUPS (475 ML)

4 tablespoons (55 g) unsalted butter

1 cup (160 g) minced onion

1 cup (240 g) ketchup

½ cup (170 g) molasses

¼ cup (60 ml) cider vinegar

¼ cup (60 ml) water

2 tablespoons (28 ml)
  Worcestershire sauce

1 tablespoon (11 g) yellow mustard

1 teaspoon kosher salt or coarse
  sea salt, plus more to taste

1 teaspoon finely ground
  black pepper

Melt the butter in a medium saucepan over medium heat. Stir in the onion, cover the pan, and sweat the onion for about 5 minutes. Uncover and add the ketchup, molasses, vinegar, water, Worcestershire sauce, mustard, salt, and black pepper. Reduce the heat to keep the sauce at a low simmer. Cook for about 20 minutes until the sauce has reduced by about one-quarter. Cool briefly and then puree in a blender. Use the sauce either warm or chilled.

What is the real secret to sauce in the heart of Texas? Barbecued meat drippings. And sometimes, some chopped meat too. Serve a meat drippings sauce warm, but keep it in the refrigerator if you don't finish it all. This is more a technique than a specific recipe because the amount of drippings, meat, and intensity of taste will affect the quantities of everything else. The sauce should be fairly thin.

CENTRAL TEXAS MEAT DRIPPINGS SAUCE

PREPARATION TIME: 10 MINUTES

YIELD DEPENDS ON YOUR DRIPPINGS

Barbecued brisket or pork drippings
  (juices and fat), warm
Finely chopped barbecued brisket
  or pork, warm
Cider vinegar and lemon juice,
  in equal amounts
Ground cayenne, enough that
  you know it's there

Mix the drippings, chopped meat, vinegar, lemon juice, and cayenne together until you hit upon a taste combination that pleases you. Serve the sauce warm. Refrigerate any remaining sauce promptly and use it within a few days.

Here's a personal favorite of mine for beef, with a little texture from caramelized bits of onion and cracked pepper. More finely ground pepper adds an appealing little afterglow at the back of your mouth. I could eat this one with a spoon.

SWEET ONION AND BLACK PEPPER SAUCE

PREPARATION TIME: 45 MINUTES

MAKES ABOUT 3 CUPS (700 ML)

4 tablespoons (55 g) unsalted butter

2 cups (320 g) minced sweet onion

¼ cup (60 g) packed light or dark
brown sugar

1 cup (240 g) ketchup

1 cup (235 ml) water

¼ cup (60 ml) cider vinegar

3 tablespoons (45 ml)
Worcestershire sauce

2 tablespoons (12 g) cracked black
peppercorns

1 tablespoon (6 g) freshly ground
black pepper

1 teaspoon kosher salt or coarse
sea salt, plus more to taste

1   Melt the butter in a saucepan over medium-low heat. Stir in the onion bits and sauté slowly until they are quite soft and beginning to turn golden, 12 to 15 minutes. Stir the onions frequently after they begin to soften. Mix in the brown sugar and cook for several minutes more to caramelize some of the onion bits.

2   Stir in the ketchup, water, vinegar, Worcestershire sauce, cracked peppercorns, black pepper, and salt and bring the sauce to a simmer. Cover and cook for 30 minutes and then allow the sauce to cool briefly. I like this sauce on the thin side so it can easily dribble off the spoon. If it's too thick, stir in a tablespoon or two (15 to 28 ml) of water. Serve warm or chilled. Store in a covered container in the refrigerator for up to 2 weeks.

The inspiration for this recipe is the sauce at The Salt Lick, a barbecue bastion just outside of Austin. The sauce actually strikes me as too sweet for Texas brisket and other beef, but I think it pairs perfectly with pork and chicken. The sauce's flavor reminds me of the sweet-sour dressing, often filled with poppy seeds, that has topped many a salad in Texas. If you don't want to bother grating an onion on the side of your cheese grater, you can substitute onion powder, but I prefer the real thing here.

SWEET-SOUR HONEY-MUSTARD BARBECUE SAUCE

PREPARATION TIME: 15 MINUTES

MAKES ABOUT 2½ CUPS (570 ML)

½ cup (120 ml) cider vinegar

½ cup (170 ml) mild-flavored honey

2 teaspoons dry mustard

2 teaspoons grated onion

2 teaspoons Worcestershire sauce

1 teaspoon sweet paprika

1 teaspoon finely ground
   black pepper

½ teaspoon garlic powder

½ teaspoon ground ginger

½ teaspoon kosher salt or coarse
   sea salt

Pinch of ground cloves

1 cup (235 ml) vegetable oil
   or sunflower oil

Combine in a food processor or blender the vinegar, honey, dry mustard, onion, Worcestershire sauce, paprika, black pepper, garlic powder, ginger, salt, and ground cloves. When well blended, with the processor still running, drizzle in the oil in a slow, steady stream until all of it is incorporated. The sauce can be used at room temperature or warmed over low heat to serve. Stored in a covered container, it keeps for several weeks in the refrigerator.

Daniel Vaughn, Texas Monthly's go-to guy for all things barbecue, was a lot smarter than me about figuring out the base of the vintage Sonny Bryant kind of barbecue sauce. I lifted the technique from him.

THIN AND TANGY BARBECUE SAUCE

PREPARATION TIME: 30 MINUTES

MAKES ABOUT 2 CUPS (475 ML)

1 medium onion, sliced

1 large lemon, sliced

4 cups (946 ml) water

1 cup (240 g) ketchup

¼ cup (60 g) packed light or dark
  brown sugar

½ cup (120 ml) white vinegar

½ cup (120 ml)
  Worcestershire sauce

1 tablespoon (19 g) kosher salt
  or coarse sea salt

1 teaspoon freshly ground
  black pepper

1   Combine the onion, lemon, and water in a large saucepan and bring to a boil over high heat. Reduce the heat to medium and reduce the mixture by one-half, about 15 minutes. Strain the liquid through a strainer into a large bowl, discard the solids, and return the liquid to the saucepan.

2   Add the ketchup, brown sugar, vinegar, Worcestershire sauce, salt, and black pepper to the pan and bring the sauce to a simmer over medium heat. Cook for about 10 minutes to blend the flavors. Use it right away or cool and refrigerate, covered, for up to several weeks.

Use this salsa with barbacoa, like the Del Rio Cachete Barbacoa on page 80 or Leg of Lamb Barbacoa on page 102. It's great on almost any type of tacos too. The tanginess of the tomatillos helps cut the richness of the smoke and meat.

ROASTED SALSA VERDE

PREPARATION TIME: 30 MINUTES

MAKES ABOUT 1½ CUPS (355 ML)

¾ pound (340 g) tomatillos,
   husks removed

5 to 6 serrano peppers or 4 jalapeño
   peppers

3 large cloves garlic

⅓ cup (5 g) roughly chopped cilantro

Juice of ½ lime

1 teaspoon kosher salt or coarse
   sea salt, plus more to taste

1 medium onion, diced fine, soaked
   in cold water to cover for about
   15 minutes

1   Preheat the broiler. Cover a baking sheet with a silicone baking mat.

2   Arrange the tomatillos, chiles, and garlic on the baking sheet. Broil for 5 to 8 minutes until all ingredients begin to darken and blister. Stir or turn them over to darken on the other side, another 5 minutes or so. Watch them carefully—you're adding flavor, not making charcoal.

3   Transfer the blackened tomatillos, chiles, and garlic to a blender, and add the cilantro, lime juice, and salt. Puree the salsa. Pour out into a bowl, stir in the onion, and taste for seasoning. The salsa should be easily spoonable. If it's thicker, stir in a tablespoon or two (15 to 28 ml) of water. Use right away or cool, cover, and refrigerate for up to several days.

If there's a single trend that's exploded in the barbecue and grilling worlds in the last decade or so, it's Asian flavors and Korean-inspired mixtures in particular.

KOREAN BARBECUE SAUCE

PREPARATION TIME: 30 MINUTES

MAKES ABOUT 2 CUPS (475 ML)

1½ cups (355 ml) *ganjang* (Korean soy sauce) or Japanese soy sauce, such as Kikkoman

½ cup (120 ml) rice vinegar

½ cup (120 g) ketchup

¼ cup (60 g) packed light brown sugar

¼ cup (25 g) thin-sliced green onions (some green portions included)

2 tablespoons (44 g) *gochujang* (Korean red pepper paste) or (28 ml) sriracha

2 tablespoons (28 ml) toasted sesame oil

1 tablespoon (6 g) minced fresh ginger

3 cloves garlic, minced

Combine the *ganjang*, vinegar, ketchup, brown sugar, green onions, *gochujang*, sesame oil, ginger, and garlic in a saucepan over medium heat. When the mixture comes to a simmer, reduce the heat to medium low and cook until reduced by about one-third, 15 to 20 minutes. Use the sauce warm, or cover and refrigerate for up to a couple of weeks. It will be best reheated.

Want an easy Asian-inspired sauce? One that also pairs across flavor profiles? Just mix some squirts of sriracha with a basic tomato-y barbecue sauce. I'd mix it with Sweet Onion and Black Pepper Sauce (page 143), but for really fast work, you can opt for a store-bought variety such as Stubbs. This is perfect with a bowl of brisket pho or ramen or a chicken spring roll.

SRIRACHA BARBECUE SAUCE

PREPARATION TIME: 5 MINUTES

MAKES ABOUT 1 CUP (235 ML)

¾ cup (175 g) tomato-based barbecue sauce

¼ cup (60 g) sriracha

Stir the barbecue sauce and sriracha together in a small bowl and serve.

Sometimes, conventional barbecue sauce, especially the tomato-based variety, just seems too heavy for a dish. By mixing some of that sauce with orange juice, oil, and vinegar, I end up with a light accompaniment for smoked pork tenderloin, chicken, seafood, or even a sweet potato salad (page 161).

CITRUS BARBECUE VINAIGRETTE

PREPARATION TIME: 15 MINUTES

MAKES 1 GENEROUS CUP (235 ML)

3 tablespoons (45 g) tomato-based
   barbecue sauce (preferably not
   super sweet or super smoky)
½ cup (120 ml) orange juice
2 teaspoons Worcestershire sauce
1 clove garlic, minced
½ cup (120 ml) vegetable oil
   or sunflower oil
Kosher salt or coarse sea salt
Freshly ground black pepper

Whisk together in a bowl the barbecue sauce, orange juice, Worcestershire sauce, and garlic. Whisk in the oil and season to taste with salt and black pepper. Use right away by drizzling over your choice of preparations or store in the refrigerator in a covered container for up to several weeks.

Hot times are ahead! Use this one judiciously, perhaps with fajitas or fish or maybe pinto beans or scrambled eggs.

CHARRED JALAPEÑO HOT SAUCE

PREPARATION TIME: 30 MINUTES, PLUS 8 HOURS' REFRIGERATION

MAKES ABOUT 1½ CUPS (355 ML)

6 large jalapeños

1 mild green chile, such as New Mexican or poblano

1 cup (235 ml) white vinegar

½ cup (120 ml) water

2 tablespoons (20 g) minced onion

2 tablespoons (17 g) pepitas (hulled pumpkin seeds)

4 cloves garlic

1½ teaspoons kosher salt or coarse sea salt

1   Char three of the jalapeños and the mild green chile directly over a stove burner or hot grill, turning to blacken on all sides. When the chiles are cool enough to handle, remove the stems and seeds but not the blackened peel. Also remove the stems and seeds from the uncharred jalapeños.

2   Transfer all of the chiles to a blender and add the vinegar, water, onion, pumpkin seeds, garlic, and salt. Puree until the sauce is smooth, which will likely take a couple of minutes. Refrigerate the sauce (you can keep it in the blender container if it fits) for at least 8 hours. After 8 hours, blend the sauce again for 1 minute and then strain it through a fine-mesh strainer into a bottle. Use immediately or refrigerate and store for later use. The hot sauce keeps for at least several weeks.

CHAPTER 10

SIDES: BEANS, GREENS, SALADS, AND MORE FROM INSIDE

Some barbecue people, who are perfectly lovely folks otherwise, entertain the flawed belief that side dishes are a waste of good stomach space. What? I have always been in the camp that thinks a taste of something else here and there, a complementary flavor or texture or temperature, allow me to enjoy and appreciate—and sometimes eat MORE—meat. Here are lots of great choices.

"We gonna get a big ol' sausage
A big plate of ranch style beans
I could eat the heart of Texas
We gonna need some brand new jeans."

—GUY CLARK,
"TEXAS COOKIN'"

Beans, nearly always pintos, sidle up to Texas barbecue nearly everywhere, whether you're eating in or eating out. At many barbecue joints, beans are offered as a free help-yourself side. The ingredients I combine here would traditionally make a dish called charro beans, but the meat would be cooked down together in the pot with the beans. However, with the deep, rich flavor of barbecued meat, I prefer to add tomatoes, chiles, and more to the beans in the form of the chunky pico de gallo so that the beans have a fresher element.

PINTOS WITH PICO

PREPARATION TIME: 15 MINUTES

COOKING TIME: ABOUT 2½ HOURS

SERVES 6 TO 8

PINTOS

1 pound (455 g) dried pinto beans, rinsed

8 cups (1.9 L) water

4 slices uncooked bacon, chopped fine, or 4 to 6 ounces (115 to 170 g) chopped barbecued brisket and fat, or 1 link smoked sausage, sliced lengthwise and then cut into thin half-moons

1 medium onion, chopped

2 to 4 cloves garlic, minced

1 tablespoon (8 g) chili powder

1 teaspoon kosher salt or coarse sea salt, plus more to taste

PICO DE GALLO

1 pound (455 g) red-ripe plum or Roma tomatoes, diced

½ cup (80 g) chopped onion

2 to 3 serrano peppers, seeded and minced

2 teaspoons olive oil

Juice of ½ lime

½ teaspoon kosher salt or coarse sea salt, plus more to taste

¼ cup (4 g) chopped cilantro

FOR THE PINTO BEANS

1   In a Dutch oven or heavy stockpot, stir together the pintos, water, bacon, onion, garlic, and chili powder. Bring the beans to a boil over high heat and then reduce the heat to a low simmer. Cook slowly, stirring the beans up from the bottom occasionally, for at least 2 hours, adding more water if the beans begin to dry out. After 2 hours, add the teaspoon of salt to the beans and cook another 15 to 30 minutes. The beans should hold their shape but be soft and just a little soupy. Serve in bowls with some of the cooking liquid.

FOR THE PICO DE GALLO

1   While the beans are cooking, prepare the Pico de Gallo. In a medium bowl, stir together the tomatoes, onion, serranos, olive oil, lime, and salt. Refrigerate the mixture for about 30 minutes.

2   Stir in the cilantro shortly before serving. Spoon the Pico de Gallo over each bowl of pintos.

VARIATIONS: Frijoles Borrachos. *For drunken beans, add 12 ounces (355 ml) light or medium-bodied beer to the beans in place of 1½ cups (355 ml) of water when beginning to cook.*

Sweet Barbecued Beans. *Eliminate the meat and pico de gallo from the recipe. Add 1 cup (235 g) barbecue sauce (such as Sweet Onion and Black Pepper Sauce, page 143), ¼ cup (60 ml) bourbon, and 2 tablespoons (30 g) brown sugar to the beans before cooking. When the beans are about 30 minutes from being ready, add ½ pound (225 g) shredded barbecued brisket or pulled pork to the beans.*

Black-Eyed Peas with Pico de Gallo. *Substitute dried black-eyed peas for the pintos and cook in the same fashion. Reduce the amount of water to 6 cups (1.4 L) since they will take less time, only about 45 minutes to 1 hour.*

You can always pull out the reliable three-bean salad recipe for a barbecue, or you could try something a little different and perhaps even more refreshing. This began as a salad from a friend in Southlake, though it seems to evolve a little each time it is made. You can make this salad several hours ahead.

CHICKPEA AND CHOPPED VEGETABLE SALAD

PREPARATION TIME: 30 MINUTES,
PLUS 30 MINUTES' REFRIGERATION

SERVES 8

DRESSING

⅓ cup (77 g) plain yogurt or (80 ml)
  buttermilk

2 tablespoons (28 ml) olive oil

2 tablespoons (28 ml) lemon juice

1 tablespoon (6 g) fresh lemon zest

1 large clove garlic, minced

½ teaspoon kosher salt or coarse
  sea salt, plus more to taste

1 large English cucumber, peeled
  if you wish, diced

1 large yellow or orange bell pepper,
  diced

1 cup (150 g) halved grape or cherry
  tomatoes, preferably a combination
  of colors

½ cup (80 g) diced red onion

½ cup (50 g) halved Kalamata olives

1 (15-ounce [425-g]) can chickpeas,
  drained and rinsed

½ cup (75 g) crumbled feta cheese

1 Prepare the dressing, whisking together the yogurt, olive oil, lemon juice, lemon zest, garlic, and salt in a large bowl. Add the cucumber, bell pepper, tomatoes, onion, olives, chickpeas, and feta to the bowl and toss the salad well to combine everything with the dressing.

2 Refrigerate for 30 minutes before serving.

Offside and Holding

Some of the oddest "side dishes" in Texas Q—the raw onions, hunks of cheese, dill pickles, white bread, saltines—actually have the most directly linked history. Central Texas barbecue evolved in meat markets that had no "real" side dishes because they weren't initially even considered restaurants by their owners or anyone else. When someone did want something extra, it had to come off the shelves, so white bread, crackers, dill pickles, onions, tomatoes, avocados, and cheese became the de facto sides. In the early years of Manhattan's biggest barbecue bash, the Big Apple BBQ Block Party in Madison Square Park, my husband and I taught a workshop about smoked Texas brisket. Everyone attending got a good laugh out of the "vegetable plate" we brought to accompany the meat. We served raw onion slices, whole fresh and pickled jalapeños, dill pickles, and basic spongy white bread slices.

This salad developed from the classic Texas cucumber salad. Use a mandoline or other slicer for best—and fastest—results. You can use sugar snaps or snow peas for the whole pea pods. It's common at farmers markets to find peas in striking purple pods. If you can find them, they look especially beautiful in this salad.

MINTY CUCUMBER-PEA SALAD

PREPARATION TIME: 45 MINUTES,
PLUS AT LEAST 2 HOURS'
REFRIGERATION

SERVES 6 TO 8

2 large English cucumbers, unpeeled,
  sliced very thin
1 small sweet onion, sliced very thin
½ cup (73 g) fresh peas
1 large handful whole sugar snap
  or snow pea pods
1½ cups (355 ml) white vinegar
¾ cup (175 ml) water
1 cup (200 g) sugar
2 tablespoons (10 g) whole
  black peppercorns
2 teaspoons kosher salt or coarse
  sea salt
1 to 2 tablespoons (6 to 12 g)
  whole fresh mint leaves

1   Place the cucumbers, onion, peas, and pea pods in a large heatproof bowl.

2   Combine in a saucepan the vinegar, water, sugar, peppercorns, and salt. Bring to a boil over high heat, stirring to dissolve sugar. When the sugar is dissolved, pour the brine over the cucumber mixture. Let cool for 20 to 30 minutes and then cover and refrigerate for at least 2 hours or up to overnight. Mix in the mint.

3   Serve the salad chilled or at room temperature using a slotted spoon.

My barbecue-indoctrinated grandkids will eat virtually any of the side dishes here, but this is the one that surprised me when they were younger. They would eat gallons of any Asian-spiced cucumbers. It's perfect on the side with any Asian-inspired barbecue, such as Korean Sesame Wings (page 59), but it's also darned fine with any rack of ribs or a pork sandwich.

ASIAN CUCUMBERS

PREPARATION TIME: 15 MINUTES, PLUS AT LEAST 1 HOUR'S REFRIGERATION

SERVES 6 TO 8

⅓ cup (80 ml) rice vinegar

2 tablespoons (28 ml) toasted sesame oil

2 teaspoons sugar

1 teaspoon kosher salt or coarse sea salt

½ teaspoon sriracha or other Asian chile paste

2 pounds (900 g) English cucumbers, peeled in stripes, then sliced in ½-inch (1.3-cm)–thick rounds

1 red jalapeño or Fresno pepper, sliced into very thin rounds

2 teaspoons toasted sesame seeds

1   In a large bowl, combine the vinegar, sesame oil, sugar, salt, and sriracha. Mix until the sugar dissolves.

2   Mix in the cucumbers and the fresh chile. Refrigerate for at least 1 hour and up to 8 hours.

3   Scatter with sesame seeds and serve.

Slaw has always been the most popular type of green salad in Texas, sometimes claiming an entire chapter in early cookbooks. This version updates the classic while still honoring the past. If you plan to spoon the slaw onto a sandwich, take the time to chop the cabbage mixture a bit more finely than the typical shreds. And of course, rather than a coleslaw vegetable mix, you are welcome to shred together half a head of cabbage with a big, fat carrot.

CREAMY COLESLAW

PREPARATION TIME: 15 MINUTES, PLUS AT LEAST 1 HOUR'S REFRIGERATION

SERVES 6

DRESSING

½ cup (115 g) plain yogurt

¼ cup (60 g) mayonnaise

3 tablespoons (45 ml) white vinegar

3 tablespoons (39 g) sugar

2 tablespoons (2 g) minced cilantro

½ teaspoon celery salt

1½ pounds (680 g) shredded coleslaw mix

Kosher salt or coarse sea salt (optional)

In a large bowl, whisk together the yogurt, mayonnaise, vinegar, sugar, cilantro, and celery salt. Add the coleslaw mix and toss to combine well.

Chill the coleslaw for at least 1 hour. Taste and add salt, if you like. Serve with a slotted spoon. I like this best within a day of making it.

VARIATION: Green Chile Coleslaw. *Before chilling, add to the coleslaw ½ to ¾ cup (60 to 80 g) chopped roasted New Mexican or poblano green chiles and an additional couple of tablespoons (2 g) chopped cilantro.*

The fascination today with fermented foods makes old German-inspired Central Texas dishes like this seem fresh again. If you like tangy vinegar-based slaws, you'll love this.

KRAUT SALAD

PREPARATION TIME: 30 MINUTES, PLUS AT LEAST
1 HOUR'S REFRIGERATION

SERVES 6

1 pound (455 g) sauerkraut

⅓ cup (55 g) minced sweet onion, such as Texas 1015,
   or ¼ cup (40 g) regular white onion

2 carrots, grated

2 medium stalks celery, chopped fine

½ small green bell pepper, chopped fine

⅔ cup (133 g) sugar

⅓ cup cider (80 ml) or white vinegar

2 tablespoons (28 ml) canola or vegetable oil

1 tablespoon (11 g) yellow mustard seeds

1 Drain the sauerkraut and then rinse and drain it again. In a large bowl, combine the drained sauerkraut with the onion, carrot, celery, and bell pepper.

2 In a small saucepan, combine the sugar and vinegar and heat until the sugar dissolves. Remove from the heat, cool briefly, and stir in the oil and mustard seeds. Pour the mixture over the kraut and toss well.

3 Refrigerate the salad at least 1 hour and up to a day ahead. Serve cold.

We tend to save peaches for dessert, but during their short summer heyday, it's a treat to combine them with savory ingredients too. Few peaches can match those from the Hill Country.

SUMMER PEACH SALAD

PREPARATION TIME: 30 MINUTES

SERVES 6 TO 8

PEACH VINAIGRETTE

1 medium peach, peeled, pitted and cut into several chunks

½ cup (120 ml) vegetable oil or sunflower oil

½ cup (120 ml) white balsamic vinegar

1 to 2 tablespoons (13 to 26 g) sugar

1 teaspoon Dijon mustard

1 teaspoon kosher salt or coarse sea salt

2 pounds (900 g) ripe but not overripe peaches, peeled
   and sliced into thin wedges

12 ounces (340 g) cucumbers, peeled, seeded, and sliced
   into half moons

⅓ cup (8 g) fresh basil leaves, torn if large

⅓ cup (12 g) fresh mint leaves

6 ounces (170 g) creamy goat cheese

2 tablespoons (18 g) toasted pine nuts

1 Prepare the Peach Vinaigrette. Combine the peach chunks, oil, vinegar, 1 tablespoon (13 g) sugar, mustard, and salt in a blender. Taste and add more sugar if needed for a bright balance. Refrigerate the vinaigrette until needed.

2 In a shallow bowl, combine the sliced peaches and cucumbers. Toss with several tablespoons of the vinaigrette. Scatter the basil and mint over and around, and crumble the goat cheese over the salad. Top with pine nuts. Serve right away.

This looks especially festive when you can pick up a mix of colored small potatoes, but you can always make it with more common red, gold, or other waxy potatoes. If all you can find are large potatoes, it's okay to cut them into bite-size chunks. It's pretty darned forgiving. Fresh basil's a good addition to this too, if you like.

RED, WHITE, AND BLUE POTATO SALAD

PREPARATION TIME: 45 MINUTES, PLUS AT LEAST 2 HOURS' REFRIGERATION

SERVES 6 TO 8

2½ pounds (1.1 kg) mixed small waxy potatoes

1 teaspoon kosher salt or coarse sea salt

4 slices uncooked bacon, chopped

⅔ cup (150 g) mayonnaise

1 tablespoon (15 g) Dijon mustard

1 teaspoon coarsely ground black pepper

¼ cup (25 g) sliced green onions (both white and green portions)

Kosher salt or coarse sea salt, to taste

1 Place the potatoes in a large saucepan and cover with cold water. Add 1 teaspoon salt. Bring to a boil over high heat and then reduce the heat to maintain a simmer. Cook until the potatoes are tender when pierced with a fork. This will depend on the size of the potatoes, but start checking after about 15 minutes of cooking. Drain and transfer the potatoes to a large bowl.

2 While the potatoes are cooking, fry the bacon. Place the bacon pieces in a skillet and turn the heat to medium low. Cook the bacon for about 3 minutes, then stir and keep cooking until crispy, about 2 more minutes. Remove the bacon with a slotted spoon and drain on paper towels. Set aside 1 tablespoon of the bacon drippings for the dressing.

3 Stir together the bacon drippings with the mayonnaise, Dijon mustard, and black pepper. Mix the dressing into the warm potatoes and then mix in the bacon and the green onions. Add salt as needed. Cover and refrigerate for at least 2 hours or up to overnight. Serve chilled.

VARIATION: **Mashed Potato Salad.** *Substitute russet potatoes for the waxy variety and once cooked, mash them roughly. Add 1 to 2 tablespoons (15 to 30 g) sweet pickle relish to the salad.*

I asked a variety of folks what they thought the most delicious over-the-top side should be with backyard barbecue. I won't tell you who said the side dish should be five brisket-sausage sandwiches. Tater tots in several forms made a strong showing. Here's how to make everybody's childhood fave as a wonderfully gooey side dish. Skip to the variation if you want to turn them into a plate of totchos instead.

TATER TOT CASSEROLE

PREPARATION TIME: 15 MINUTES

COOKING TIME: 45 TO 50 MINUTES

SERVES 6

1 pound (455 g) frozen tater tots

¾ cup (173 g) sour cream

½ cup (120 ml) ranch dressing

6 ounces (170 g) mild Cheddar cheese, shredded

4 cooked bacon slices, crumbled

2 green onions, sliced thin (both white and green portions)

Fresh or pickled jalapeños, sliced

Kosher salt or coarse sea salt, to taste

1 Preheat the oven to 350°F (180°C, or gas mark 4). Oil a shallow medium baking dish.

2 Mix the tater tots, sour cream, ranch dressing, Cheddar cheese, bacon, and green onions together in a large bowl, adding jalapeños and salt to taste. Spoon into the prepared baking dish.

3 Bake for 45 to 50 minutes, until the casserole is bubbly and golden brown. Serve hot.

VARIATION: Loaded Totchos. *On a small baking sheet lined with parchment, bake the tots plain at 425°F (220°C, or gas mark 7) for about 10 minutes until brown and crisp. Add all of the other ingredients as toppings and return to the oven for 2 to 3 minutes, just until the cheese melts and the sauce is bubbly. Watch carefully so that the cheese doesn't turn to rubber. As with nachos, eat with your fingers for the full experience.*

Sweet potatoes make a hearty salad, but this one, with a lively vinaigrette, doesn't taste heavy.

SWEET POTATO SALAD WITH SRIRACHA BARBECUE VINAIGRETTE

PREPARATION TIME: 30 MINUTES, PLUS AT LEAST 1 HOUR'S REFRIGERATION

SERVES 6

2 to 2¼ pounds (0.9 to 1 kg) sweet potatoes, peeled and cut into bite-size chunks

2 teaspoons kosher salt or coarse sea salt

SRIRACHA BARBECUE VINAIGRETTE

3 tablespoons (45 g) tomato-based barbecue sauce (preferably not super sweet or super smoky)

1 tablespoon (15 ml) sriracha

½ cup (120 ml) vegetable oil or sunflower oil

Kosher salt or coarse sea salt and freshly ground black pepper, to taste

1 large yellow bell pepper, seeded and diced

1 stalk celery, chopped fine

4 green onions, sliced thin, some green tops included

1   Place the sweet potatoes in a large saucepan and cover by a couple of inches (5 cm) with salted water. Cook the sweet potatoes over medium-high heat until tender, 10 to 12 minutes. Drain the sweet potatoes, rinse them in cold water, and drain again. Set them aside to cool briefly.

2   In a small bowl, whisk together the barbecue sauce and sriracha. Whisk in the oil and season to taste with salt and black pepper.

3   Combine the sweet potatoes, bell pepper, celery, and green onions in a large bowl, mixing lightly. Pour in about two-thirds of the dressing and mix again. Add more dressing if you wish.

4   Cover and refrigerate for at least 1 hour or up to overnight. Serve chilled. The salad keeps well for several days.

My first Mexican-style elote *was in one of the plazas of Puerta Vallarta at least three decades ago. It was a Sunday night, when local families came out and promenaded or simply sat on park benches and low walls and chatted with friends. I was still very nervous about eating from a street food stand, but it wasn't meat, the aroma was scintillating, and corn was oh-so-familiar to a girl originally from Illinois. I took the plunge and have been eating street food worldwide ever since. This salad takes inspiration from the now-ubiquitous beloved street corn style. Lots of us north of the border call this* elotes, *but that actually refers to corn on the cob. More properly, kernels sliced off the cob are* esquites. *Call it what you will. Just call me when it's ready.*

MEXICAN STREET CORN SALAD

PREPARATION TIME: 30 MINUTES,
PLUS AT LEAST 30 MINUTES'
REFRIGERATION

SERVES 6 TO 8

3 tablespoons (45 ml) vegetable
  or sunflower oil
5 medium ears corn, shucked and
  kernels sliced off the cobs
  (3 to 3½ cups [442 to 539 g]
  corn kernels)
2 tablespoons (28 g) mayonnaise
2 tablespoons (30 g) Mexican-style
  crema or sour cream
Juice of 1 large lime
1 teaspoon chili powder
½ cup (75 g) crumbled queso fresco
  or feta cheese
1 serrano or jalapeño pepper,
  seeded and finely chopped
¼ cup (4 g) chopped cilantro
2 green onions, white and green
  portions, sliced into very
  thin rounds

1 Heat the oil in a large skillet over medium-high heat. Add the corn kernels and sauté until slightly browned in spots, 5 to 8 minutes. Scrape the corn into a large bowl and let it cool briefly.

2 Add the mayonnaise, crema, lime juice, and chili powder. Mix well. Refrigerate for at least 30 minutes.

3 Shortly before serving, gently mix in the queso fresco, jalapeño, cilantro, and green onions. Serve.

"Hot corn, cold corn,
bring along the demijohn . . ."

—TRADITIONAL SONG
AS SUNG BY ROBERT EARL KEEN

The best creamed corn I ever tasted was at Killen's Barbecue in Pearland, outside of Houston.
More recently, Ronnie Killen opened Killen's STQ in Houston and added the corn to the big city
menu too. It made it a lot easier to get a dish of it, which might not be the best idea for my
waistline. This isn't Killen's recipe but that one completely occupied my mind as I worked on this
version. Part of the recipe's success owes to the scraping of the "milk" from the corn cobs after
the kernels have been sliced off.

CREAMED CORN

PREPARATION TIME:1 HOUR

SERVES 6

6 ears fresh sweet corn
2 cups (475 ml) half-and-half
6 tablespoons (85 g) salted butter
¾ to 1½ teaspoons sugar
½ teaspoon kosher salt or coarse
   sea salt, plus more to taste
⅛ teaspoon ground white pepper

1   Slice the kernels off each cob, using a sharp knife. Using the dull top side of the knife, scrape down each ear again, pressing against the cob to release the thick semi-liquid corn cream. Reserve both corn kernals and cobs.

2   Pour the half-and-half in a large saucepan and add the corn cobs. You may need to halve the cobs to fit or leave out a section or two of cob if it's too full, but you want as many as will fit to flavor the half-and-half. Bring to a bare simmer over medium heat. Reduce the heat to low and cook for about 20 minutes, reducing the liquid to the thickness of heavy cream and infusing the half-and-half with the flavor of the cobs.

3   Meanwhile, in a medium saucepan, melt the butter over medium heat. Add the corn kernels, reduce the heat to low, and cook for about 15 minutes, stirring a time or two.

4   Remove the corn cobs from the half-and-half and scrape any clinging half-and-half back into the pan. Discard the cobs.

5   Spoon one-quarter of the corn into the half-and-half mixture and puree until smooth with an immersion blender. (Alternatively, transfer one-quarter of the corn and the half-and-half to the container of a regular blender, blend, and then return to the pan.) Stir in the remaining corn. Add ¾ teaspoon sugar, ½ teaspoon salt, and the white pepper. Simmer until thickened and heated through, about 10 minutes more. Adjust the seasoning, adding more sugar or salt if you wish. Don't overdo the sugar. It should heighten the natural sweetness of the corn rather than make it taste like candy. Serve hot.

Long-cooked collard greens show up on many of the African-American barbecue menus but are certainly not limited to them. Substitute mustard greens if you prefer.

A MESS OF COLLARDS

PREPARATION TIME: 30 MINUTES

COOKING TIME: ABOUT 2 HOURS

SERVES 8

8 cups (1.9 L) water

1 smoked ham hock (about 1 pound [455 g])

3 medium onions, chopped

1 green bell pepper, seeded and chopped

1 red bell pepper, seeded and chopped

1 yellow bell pepper, seeded and chopped

3 cloves garlic, minced

2 teaspoons coarsely ground black pepper

1 teaspoon kosher salt or coarse sea salt, plus more to taste

3 to 3½ pounds (1.4 to 1.6 kg) collard greens, tough stems removed and leaves roughly chopped or torn

1 In a stockpot or other large pot, combine the water, ham hock, onions, bell peppers, garlic, black pepper, and salt. Bring to a boil over high heat and then reduce the heat to maintain a simmer and cook for about 15 minutes. Add the collards to the pot. Cover and cook for about 2 hours until very tender.

2 Remove the ham hock with a slotted spoon. When the meat is cool enough to handle, shred it into small bits, discarding the fat and bone. Return the meat to the pot. Reheat briefly before serving with some of the liquid, or pot likker, which is full of vitamins. The greens can be made a day ahead, if you wish. Leftovers keep well, refrigerated, for several days.

The apple-like crunch of jicama is a welcome pairing with melon. If you haven't shopped for jicama before, it looks like a bulbous brown thing, sometimes almost football-like. Often, it's sold in halves or wedges so you'll see some of the creamy interior flesh. I prefer honeydew for this salad because it has a slight bit of firmness behind its sweetness, but for a change, mix it up with cantaloupe or a combination of melons.

JICAMA AND HONEYDEW SALAD

PREPARATION TIME: 30 MINUTES

SERVES 6 TO 8

DRESSING

¼ cup (120 ml) fresh lime juice

2 teaspoons fresh lime zest

2 tablespoons (40 ml) agave syrup
  or mild-flavored honey

2 tablespoons (26 g) sugar

1 teaspoon smoked paprika

¼ teaspoon onion powder

¼ teaspoon kosher salt or coarse
  sea salt, plus more to taste

½ cup (120 ml) vegetable or
  sunflower oil

12 ounces (340 g) jicama, peeled
  and cut into bite-size cubes

1 medium to large honeydew, peeled
  and cut into bite-size cubes

1 large avocado, diced

⅓ cup (45 g) Marcona almonds

1 Prepare the dressing. In a food processor or blender, combine the lime juice, lime zest, agave syrup, sugar, paprika, onion powder, and salt. When well mixed, drizzle the oil in while continuing to process or blend. The dressing will thicken. Refrigerate until needed.

2 Combine the jicama and honeydew in a large bowl and toss with several tablespoons of dressing. Scatter with avocado chunks and almonds. Drizzle with more dressing as desired and serve.

Maybe only Hawaii equals Texas in its love of macaroni salad. Mind you, we're not talking some food magazine pasta salad. No, I mean the old-style salad that remains popular at joints and cafes and, most certainly, at picnics. This particular one hailed originally from the Hicks family in Amarillo. To give this a little extra zip, I like to use a pickle relish with some heat along with the sweet, such as Wickle's.

MACARONI SALAD

PREPARATION TIME: 30 MINUTES

SERVES 6 TO 8

¾ pound (340 g) dry elbow macaroni

½ cup (115 g) mayonnaise

¼ cup (60 g) sour cream
  or plain yogurt

⅔ cup (163 g) sweet pickle relish

1 cup (130 g) baby peas, fresh
  or frozen and thawed

8 ounces (225 g) mild or medium
  Cheddar, finely diced

1 green bell pepper, finely diced

½ red bell pepper, finely diced

¼ cup (30 g) minced celery

3 green onions, sliced into thin
  rounds, some of the green
  tops included

Kosher salt or coarse sea salt and
  ground white pepper, to taste

Cook the macaroni according to package directions and drain it. Spoon the macaroni into a large bowl and mix with the mayonnaise and sour cream. Add the relish, peas, Cheddar, bell peppers, celery, green onions, and salt and white pepper to taste. Toss well to combine. Cover and refrigerate for at least 1 hour and up to a day. Serve chilled.

VARIATION: **Bacon-and-Mac Salad.** *Depending upon the meatiness of the meal in other courses and who you're cooking for, you might add four crisp-cooked bacon slices, crumbled, to make this heartier.*

A generation or two ago, an avocado-grapefruit salad was arguably the most popular "company" salad you could find on Texas tables. Popularized by Neiman Marcus chef Helen Corbitt, who was an early advocate for local ingredients, it made use of Rio Grande Valley fruits. Corbitt tied them together with a sweet-sour dressing that paid homage to the German traditions of the state. The tanginess of the grapefruit makes it a fine accompaniment to a plate of smoked food, and the salad's shades of red and green brighten up an otherwise brown meal. Fennel slices and the dressing's poppy seeds offer a nice bit of texture. If you haven't bought poppy seeds before, you'll find them with the bottled spices in a store's baking section.

AVOCADO-GRAPEFRUIT-FENNEL SALAD

PREPARATION TIME: 30 MINUTES

SERVES 6

POPPY SEED DRESSING

½ cup (120 ml) white or cider vinegar

2½ to 3 tablespoons (50 to 60 g) mild-flavored honey

½ teaspoon Dijon mustard

¼ teaspoon onion powder

¼ teaspoon kosher salt or coarse sea salt, plus more to taste

½ cup (120 ml) canola or vegetable oil

2 teaspoons poppy seeds

3 large ruby red grapefruits, such as Rio Star, peeled and sectioned

1 small fennel bulb, trimmed and sliced vertically into thin ribbons

2 large avocados, cut into about 10 slices each

Butter lettuce leaves or shredded romaine

1 In a food processor or blender, combine the vinegar, honey (use the smaller amount if the grapefruit is really sweet), mustard, onion powder, and salt. When well mixed, drizzle the oil in while continuing to process or blend. The dressing will thicken. Scrape into a bowl and stir in the poppy seeds. (The dressing can be kept, covered and refrigerated, for up to a week.)

2 Shortly before you plan to eat, arrange the grapefruit sections, fennel slices, and avocado slices neatly on a platter and tuck lettuce around the edges. Drizzle the dressing over the salad or pass the dressing for each person to dress their own.

Grits gussied up with a combo of jalapeños and cheese are pretty common all over Texas these days. I take the mixture a step further, using prepared pimiento cheese. If you need speed, you can substitute quick-cooking (5-minute) grits, reducing their cooking time and the quantity of water needed, but please avoid pablum-like instant grits.

RED CHILE–PIMIENTO CHEESE GRITS

PREPARATION TIME: 45 MINUTES

COOKING TIME: 45 MINUTES TO
1 HOUR

SERVES 6

6 cups (1.4 L) water

1 teaspoon kosher salt or coarse
sea salt

1 tablespoon (8 g) ground medium-
heat red chile, such as New
Mexican or ancho

1 cup (140 g) coarse-ground grits
or polenta

2 tablespoons (28 g) unsalted butter

8 ounces (225 g, about 1 cup)
pimiento cheese

2 large eggs, lightly beaten

1   Preheat the oven to 300°F (150°C, or gas mark 2). Oil a medium baking dish, something like 9 × 13 inches (23 × 33 cm).

2   Bring the water to a boil in a large saucepan. When the water reaches a rolling boil, add the salt and red chile. Add the grits gradually, a handful at a time, stirring them in before adding the next handful. Reduce the heat to maintain a bare simmer and cook the grits until thick and soft, about 30 minutes. Give the grits a stir up from the bottom every few minutes, and more frequently toward the end, to avoid scorching.

3   Remove the grits from the heat and stir in the butter, pimento cheese, and eggs. Scrape the mixture into the prepared pan. Bake for 45 to 55 minutes until lightly set and slightly brown. Let the grits sit at room temperature for at least 10 minutes and then cut into soft-textured wedges or squares.

Stephan Pyles, superstar Dallas chef and barbecue fan, created these cornbread "muffins" for one of his early restaurants, Star Canyon. I loved everything Stephan served at Star Canyon but have never forgotten these deep-blue individual breads, served piping hot. If you want to serve them frequently, you might want to acquire a set of cast-iron star molds for cornbread, though you can make the individual breads in muffin tins too. I recommend serving them, whatever their shape, with a generous smear of honey butter. Heavenly.

BLUE CORN STARS

PREPARATION TIME: 30 MINUTES

COOKING TIME: 20 TO 25 MINUTES

MAKES 8 TO 10 MUFFINS

8 tablespoons (112 g)
   unsalted butter

8 tablespoons (100 g)
   vegetable shortening

4 serrano peppers, seeded
   and minced

3 cloves garlic, minced

1¼ cup (175 g) blue cornmeal,
   preferably, or yellow cornmeal

1 cup (125 g) all-purpose flour

2 tablespoons (26 g) sugar

1 teaspoon baking powder

1½ teaspoons kosher salt or coarse
   sea salt

3 large eggs

1¼ cups (285 ml) whole milk,
   at room temperature

1   Preheat the oven to 400°F (200°C, or gas mark 8). Spray a star-shaped corn muffin molds or muffin tins with nonstick spray.

2   In a small saucepan, combine the butter and shortening. Melt over low heat then add the serrano and garlic. Sauté for about 5 minutes until soft. Set aside to cool briefly.

3   Sift together into a large mixing bowl the cornmeal, flour, sugar, baking powder, and salt and set aside. Whisk the eggs in a medium bowl and then add to them the melted butter mixture and milk. Scrape the liquid ingredients into the dry ingredients and whisk just until smooth. Do not overmix.

4   Spoon the batter equally into the molds or muffin tins. Bake on the center rack of the oven for 20 to 25 minutes until lightly browned and springy to the touch. Cool in the tins on a baking rack for about 5 minutes. Then, run a small knife around the edges of each muffin and transfer to a basket. Serve warm.

CHAPTER 11

HAPPY ENDINGS: A HANDFUL OF SWEET FINISHES

Sweet follows smoke the way amorous eyes follow tight jeans, on guys or gals. While in barbecue joints of the past, a couple of those red-dyed peanut patties were pretty much the dessert of choice, today's pitmasters are making the finish of the meal every bit as interesting as what went in the pit. Some desserts have smoke added to them too. Here, I'm sharing great versions of slightly more conventional choices, but ones that I hope you'll find absolutely delectable to wrap up a meal.

Given the summer temperatures and additional heat radiating from your smoker, nothing may wrap up a barbecued meal better than ice cream. Here's a true Texas favorite.

BUTTER-PECAN ICE CREAM

PREPARATION TIME: 30 MINUTES,
PLUS 1 HOUR'S REFRIGERATION,
PLUS FREEZING

MAKES ABOUT 1 QUART (946 ML)

1½ cups (165 g) chopped
    raw pecans

3 tablespoons (42 g) unsalted butter

1 cup (225 g) packed light brown
    sugar, divided

3 cups (700 ml) half-and-half

4 large egg yolks

¼ teaspoon table salt

2 teaspoons pure vanilla extract

1   Toast the pecans in a heavy skillet over medium heat until fragrant, about 5 minutes. Pour half of the pecans into a medium saucepan. Return the skillet with the remaining pecans to the stovetop over medium heat and stir in the butter and 2 tablespoons (30 g) of the brown sugar. Stir continually while the sugar and butter melt. Remove from the heat immediately once melted and set aside.

2   Pour the half-and-half into the saucepan with the toasted pecans. Whisk in the egg yolks, salt, and the remaining brown sugar. Place over medium-low heat and stir up from the bottom, frequently, until the custard thickens, about 10 to 12 minutes. Do not boil. Stir in the vanilla and remove the pan from the heat. Pour the custard through a strainer into a medium bowl, and discard the strained pecans. (I feed them to my chickens.) Refrigerate the custard for at least a couple of hours and up to overnight.

3   Transfer the custard to an ice cream maker and freeze according to the manufacturer's directions. When the ice cream is nearly ready, stir the brown sugar–coated pecans into the ice cream and finish churning. Put the ice cream into a freezer-safe container, cover it, transfer it to the freezer for at least 1 hour. The ice cream is best eaten within several days.

I've written enough peach cobbler recipes to put together a book on just that topic. It's as Texan as Texan can be, but it's time for a more refreshing take on the favorite fruit of Central Texas. (See almost any other book I've written to find a cobbler recipe or use a favorite from your family or another book.) I'm here to tell you that when you've been outside barbecuing, the peach dessert that may satisfy you most might just be this sorbet, which isn't much more than pureed and frozen fruit. Judge the amount of sugar needed after tasting the peaches for sweetness.

PEACH SORBET

PREPARATION TIME: 15 MINUTES,
PLUS 1 HOUR'S REFRIGERATION,
PLUS FREEZING

MAKES 1 QUART (946 ML)

2½ to 2¾ pounds (1.1 to 1.2 kg)
    ripe juicy peaches, sliced in half
    and pitted
¾ cup (150 g) sugar, adjusted to
    taste based on the sweetness
    of your peaches
2 teaspoons fresh lemon juice
Several drops pure vanilla extract

1   Puree—really puree—the ingredients together in a food processor. Pour through a fine strainer, pushing on the peach pulp to get as much juice as possible. Refrigerate until chilled, at least 1 hour and up to a day.

2   Freeze the sorbet in an ice cream maker according to the manufacturer's directions. Served directly from the ice cream maker, the sorbet will be a bit soft. If you like it firmer, place it in a covered freezer-safe container and freeze for several hours. The flavor is best within the first couple of days.

Invest in some inexpensive frozen pop molds to make these Mexican-style popsicles. They're easy to toss together whenever you, the pitmaster, or the kids need a blast of cool refreshment. These two-toned paletas are inspired by the big clear jugs of aguas frescas *seen all over Texas fairs and* ferias.

MANGO-WATERMELON PALETAS

PREPARATION TIME: 30 MINUTES, PLUS FREEZING

MAKES ABOUT 8 FROZEN POPS

1½ cups (355 ml) mango or mango-orange juice or nectar

Juice of ½ lime

1½ cups (225 g) seedless watermelon chunks

1 to 2 teaspoons sugar

1   Stir the mango juice and lime juice together and set aside half. Using half of the mango-lime juice, divide the juice equally among 8 pop molds. Tap the molds on the counter to eliminate any air pockets. Cover the mold with the lids that come with the it. (Some lids form their own handles for the pops. Others generally include sticks so, if needed, insert the sticks into the slit opening in each lid.) Freeze until lightly set, at least 30 minutes.

2   Puree the watermelon with the sugar in a blender. Pour the watermelon juice into the molds over the first layer of mango, dividing all of it among the molds. Tap the molds again on the counter to eliminate air bubbles. Freeze again until lightly set, at least 30 minutes.

3   Top off each paleta with an equal portion of remaining mango-lime juice. (If you have any juice left, just drink it—cook's treat.) Tap on the counter again. Freeze the molds until firmly set, at least 1 more hour. The paletas will keep for at least a week before their flavor fades.

4   To unmold the paletas, gently squeeze the bottom or sides of each mold with one hand while pulling on the stick with the other. If they don't come out easily, dunk the bottoms of the molds in hot water for just a second or two, then try again. Serve and slurp immediately.

You'll find either bread pudding or banana pudding on the majority of Texas barbecue joint menus. Both slide down easy after a meal of fine Q, whether you're out or at home. For a world-class banana pudding recipe, I recommend the one from Pecan Lodge in Dallas, found online. Here's a less well-known recipe from the best barbecue bastion out on the Llano Estacado, Evie Mae's Pit Barbeque, just outside of Lubbock in Wolfforth. Conveniently, it's on my way to just about everywhere I visit in Texas, and I can get there easily by lunch from my New Mexico home. It's a family operation for Arnis and Mallory Robbins, who named the restaurant after their daughter Evie Mae. This recipe and many others of theirs are gluten-free since Arnis has celiac disease. They also make some awesome barbecue pits as their side business.

EVIE MAE'S CORNBREAD PUDDING AND BOURBON SAUCE

PREPARATION TIME: 30 MINUTES

COOKING TIME: 30 MINUTES

SERVES 8

3 generous cups (350 g) cubed cornbread (see note below)
2 cups (400 g) sugar
2½ cups (570 ml) whole milk
2 large eggs
2 tablespoons (30 ml) pure vanilla extract
1 teaspoon ground cinnamon
1 cup (110 g) unsalted pecan pieces

BOURBON SAUCE
8 tablespoons (112 g) salted butter
½ cup (100 g) sugar
½ cup (120 ml) heavy whipping cream
3 tablespoons (45 ml) bourbon

1   Preheat the oven to 350°F (180°C, or gas mark 4). Grease a 9-inch (23 cm)–square baking dish.

2   Place the cornbread in the baking dish. Combine the 2 cups (400 g) sugar, milk, eggs, vanilla, cinnamon, and pecans in a bowl and then pour the mixture evenly over the cornbread. Push the cornbread down a bit so that every bit is moistened. Cover the pan with foil and bake it for about 30 minutes. Uncover and continue baking for about 5 more minutes until the top is browned in spots.

3   While the pudding bakes, prepare the Bourbon Sauce. Combine the butter, ½ cup sugar (100 g), cream, and bourbon in a saucepan and warm over medium heat. Cook for about 5 minutes until the butter is melted. Keep warm until the pudding is ready.

4   Spoon the warm pudding into bowls. Give the sauce a good whisk and pour equal portions over each serving.

NOTE: *You can make this with any cornbread recipe. The one Evie Mae's uses is gluten free, as is this one, if you want to try it. First, preheat the oven to 425°F (220°C, or gas mark 7) and place an oiled 9-inch (23 cm) skillet in the oven to heat as well. Whisk together 2 cups (475 ml) buttermilk, 2 large eggs, and ⅛ teaspoon pure vanilla extract. Combine in another bowl 2 cups (280 g) polenta cornmeal, 1 tablespoon (13 g) sugar, and 1 teaspoon each of salt and baking soda. Add the buttermilk mixture and 4 tablespoons (55 g) melted salted butter to the dry ingredients. Scrape the batter into the hot skillet and bake for 15 to 18 minutes until lightly browned and just set. Cool and cut into cubes for the cornbread pudding.*

Cousin to the margarita, a paloma showcases grapefruit juice with tequila. Equally sassy, the drink's a good jumping-off point to create a frozen pie, one you can make with ingredients that are easy to keep on hand. Red grapefruit juice concentrate gives you the prettiest color, but any will do. On a hot Texas day, it's like air conditioning you can eat.

FROZEN PALOMA PIE

PREPARATION TIME: 30 MINUTES, PLUS AT LEAST 1 HOUR'S FREEZING

COOKING TIME: 10 MINUTES

MAKES A 9-INCH (23 CM) PIE

CRUST

¾ cup (110 g) salted pretzels, roughly crumbled

½ cup (70 g) graham cracker crumbs

2 tablespoons (26 g) sugar

4 tablespoons (56 g) salted butter, melted

FILLING

1 (6-ounce [170 g]) can frozen red grapefruit juice concentrate, thawed

1 (8-ounce [225 g]) container frozen whipped topping, thawed

¼ cup (60 ml) 100% blue agave silver tequila

1 tablespoon (15 ml) Triple Sec or other orange liqueur

Fresh grapefruit segments, optional for serving

1 Preheat the oven to 350°F (180°C, or gas mark 4). Grease a 9-inch (23 cm) pie pan.

2 Prepare the crust. Combine the pretzels, graham cracker crumbs, and sugar in a large bowl, then stir in the butter until moistened. Press the crust evenly into the pie pan, using the back of a spoon to smooth it. Bake for about 10 minutes, until lightly colored and set. Let cool to room temperature.

3 Prepare the filling. Whisk together the grapefruit juice concentrate, whipped topping, tequila, and Triple Sec in a large bowl. Spoon the filling into the pie crust and freeze until set, at least 1 hour.

4 Garnish with fresh grapefruit segments, if you wish, then slice and serve.

This custard pie may sound odd, but it's been a Southern—and specifically Texan—favorite for generations. Sometimes called a "deprivation" pie because it could be made when no fruit was on hand, it has a charm all its own and can be found on the menus of many barbecue establishments. The gentle tang of its custard filling is a perfect foil for smoky flavors, kind of like the slight tang of goat cheese over cow's milk cheese. Serve with a few berries on the side, if you like.

BUTTERMILK PIE

PREPARATION TIME: 45 MINUTES, PLUS AT LEAST 30 MINUTES COOLING

COOKING TIME: 35 TO 45 MINUTES

MAKES A 9-INCH (23 CM) PIE

SINGLE FLAKY PIE CRUST

1¼ cup (156 g) all-purpose flour

½ teaspoon table salt

3 tablespoons (42 g) unsalted butter, chilled

3 tablespoons (39 g) lard or vegetable shortening

3 to 4 tablespoons (45 to 60 ml) ice water

FILLING

1 cup (200 g) sugar

3 large eggs

3 tablespoons (23 g) all-purpose flour

4 tablespoons (55 g) unsalted butter, softened

2 tablespoons (28 ml) fresh lemon juice

2 teaspoons lemon zest

1 teaspoon pure vanilla extract

1½ cups (355 ml) low-fat buttermilk

Ground nutmeg, for topping

1   Preheat the oven to 400°F (200°C, or gas mark 6). Grease a 9-inch (23 cm) pie pan.

2   To make the pie crust, combine the flour, salt, 3 tablespoons (42 g) butter, and lard in a food processor using short pulses to mix lightly until most of the mixture is in pea-size crumbles. Add 3 tablespoons (45 ml) of the ice water and process just until the dough holds together. Add the remaining water if needed to have a cohesive dough.

3   On a floured surface, roll out the dough into a circle just larger than a 9-inch (23 cm) pie pan. Roll from the center outwards, avoiding rerolling more than necessary. Drape the dough over the rolling pin, center the crust over the pan, and drop it gently into place. Crimp the edge decoratively. With a fork, prick the dough in the bottom of the pan in several places. Refrigerate the crust for about 15 minutes.

4   Parbake the pie crust for 5 to 7 minutes, just until it loses its raw look. Remove it to a cooling rack and reduce the oven temperature 350°F (180°C, or gas mark 4).

5   To make the filling, use an electric mixer to beat together the sugar and eggs at medium speed until well blended and a couple of shades lighter yellow. Mix in the flour just until it disappears into the sugar-egg mixture. Add the 4 tablespoons (55 g) butter, lemon juice and zest, and vanilla and mix again. Add the buttermilk and mix until the filling is well blended.

6   Pour the filling into the prepared crust. Sprinkle generously with nutmeg. Bake the pie for 30 to 35 minutes until filling appears lightly but fully set. There should still be just the slightest touch of jiggle at the center.

7   Let the pie sit on a cooling rack for at least 30 minutes to cool and set up before slicing. Cover and refrigerate any leftovers, although the pie is best enjoyed the day it's made.

In African-American-owned barbecue restaurants, in particular, I always hope for a creamy sweet potato pie finish to the meal. Here's my take on this luscious dessert.

SWEET POTATO PIE

PREPARATION TIME: 45 MINUTES

COOKING TIME: ABOUT 45 MINUTES

MAKES A 9-INCH (23 CM) PIE

SINGLE FLAKY PIE CRUST

1¼ cup (156 g) all-purpose flour

½ teaspoon fine sea salt

3 tablespoons (42 g) unsalted butter, chilled

3 tablespoons (39 g) lard or vegetable shortening

3 to 4 tablespoons (45 to 60 ml) ice water

FILLING

1 pound (455 g) sweet potatoes, baked and peeled, warm

4 tablespoons (55 g) salted butter

14 ounce (425 ml) can sweetened condensed milk

2 large eggs

1 teaspoon pure vanilla extract

1 teaspoon freshly grated orange zest

1 teaspoon ground nutmeg

½ teaspoon ground cinnamon

1. Preheat the oven to 400°F (200°C, or gas mark 6). Grease a 9-inch (23 cm) pie pan.

2. To make the pie crust, combine the flour, salt, 3 tablespoons (42 g) butter, and lard in a food processor using short pulses to mix lightly. Add 3 tablespoons (45 ml) of the ice water and process just until the dough holds together. Add the remaining water if needed to have a cohesive dough.

3. On a floured surface, roll out the dough into a circle just larger than a 9-inch (23 cm) pie pan. Roll from the center outwards, avoiding rerolling more than necessary. Drape the dough over the rolling pin, center the crust over the pan, and drop it gently into place. Crimp the edge decoratively. With a fork, prick the dough in the bottom of the pan in several places. Refrigerate the crust for about 15 minutes.

4. Beat together the sweet potatoes and 4 tablespoons (55 g) butter in the bowl with an electric mixer at medium-high speed until smooth. Stop the mixer and scrape down the sides of the bowl. Add the sweetened condensed milk, eggs, vanilla, orange zest, nutmeg, and cinnamon and beat well for about 1 more minute.

5. Pour the filling into the prepared crust. Bake the pie for 40 to 45 minutes until the filling appears lightly but fully set.

6. Let the pie sit on a cooling rack for at least 30 minutes to cool and set up before slicing. Cover and refrigerate any leftovers, although the pie is best enjoyed the day it's made.

Don't you love a pie you can pick up in your hand? It's so totally in keeping with a barbecue meal where you likely need no fork for the main dish either. These have a tender crust that tastes like a cross between a pie crust and a sugar cookie.

STRAWBERRY–CREAM CHEESE SWEET DOUGH HAND PIES

PREPARATION TIME: 1 HOUR

COOKING TIME: ABOUT 15 MINUTES

MAKES 8 HAND PIES

CRUST

2 cups (250 g) all-purpose flour

2 teaspoons baking powder

½ teaspoon table salt

8 tablespoons (112 g) salted butter, softened

2 tablespoons (26 g) lard or vegetable shortening

¼ cup plus 2 tablespoons (76 g) sugar

1 large egg

¼ cup (60 ml) whole milk or half-and-half

½ teaspoon pure vanilla extract

FILLING

4 ounces (115 g) cream cheese, softened

1 cup (320 g) strawberry preserves

1 to 2 tablespoons (15 to 28 ml) whole milk or half-and-half

Turbinado sugar

VARIATION: Blueberry–Cream Cheese Hand Pies. *Replace the strawberry preserves with blueberry jam.*

1 Prepare the dough, first stirring together the flour, baking powder, and salt in a medium bowl.

2 Cream together the butter, lard, and sugar in a large bowl, beating until fluffy and light, about 5 minutes with an electric mixer at high speed. Beat in the egg, milk, and vanilla and then add about half of the flour mixture, beating it in completely before adding the rest. Stop as needed to scrape down the sides of the bowl. Scrape the dough from the bowl and pat it out into 2-inch (5 cm)–thick disks. Wrap the disks in plastic and refrigerate for at least 20 minutes. (The dough can be made ahead and refrigerated for up to several days. Let it sit only briefly at room temperature before proceeding.)

3 While the dough chills, prepare the filling. Combine the cream cheese and strawberry preserves in a small bowl. (The filling can be made a day ahead, covered, and refrigerated.)

4 When ready to bake the hand pies, preheat the oven to 375°F (190°C, or gas mark 5). Arrange a silicone mat or baking parchment on a baking sheet.

5 Take just one dough disk out at a time. Roll out the dough on a floured surface to about ⅓ inch (8 mm) thickness. Cut the dough into squares about 6 inches (15 cm) across or cut out 5- to 6-inch (13 to 15 cm) rounds. (I use the lid of a canister for this size.) Spoon 1½ to 2 tablespoons (15 to 30 g) of the filling in the middle of each section of dough and then fold one side of the dough over the other and pinch around the edges to make a tight seal. (A few crackles in the dough's surface are not uncommon, but if it cracks badly when forming into pies, reroll the dough a bit thicker.)

6 Crimp the edges neatly with the tines of a fork. Make a couple of ½-inch (1.3 cm) slashes in the top of each pie to let steam escape. Transfer the pies to the prepared baking sheet with a dough scraper or wide spatula to avoid tearing the dough. Brush each pie lightly across the top with milk, then sprinkle with turbinado sugar. Repeat with the remaining dough and filling.

7 Arrange the hand pies at least ½ inch (1.3 cm) apart on the baking sheet. Bake for 13 to 15 minutes until lightly browned. Cool the pies on the baking sheet for several minutes and then finish cooling them on cooling racks. Serve warm or at room temperature.

Texas has always had sweet spot for congealed Jell-O salads. To me, that makes an easy leap to almond "jelly," the cooling finish to some Chinese or Southeast Asian meals. Jellies have been thickened traditionally with agar-agar, made from seaweed, which is popular these days among vegetarians and vegans. Since I seriously doubt that many vegans have picked up this meat-o-rama of a book, I call for unflavored gelatin, which is more easily found in supermarkets and has more predictable results. Fresh lychees are showing up in more markets in summer months, and if you see them, by all means, use them. To me, they have a berry-like undertone to their flavor that pairs perfectly with strawberries or raspberries, in particular. The shell-like skin and large seed of fresh lychees are easy to remove. If you come across fresh rambutans, a lychee cousin, they can be used too.

ALMOND JELLY WITH BERRIES AND LYCHEES

PREPARATION TIME: 30 MINUTES, PLUS AT LEAST 2 HOURS' REFRIGERATION

SERVES 6

2 tablespoons (14 g) unflavored gelatin

2 cups (475) warm water

¼ cup (50 g) sugar

½ cup (120 ml) sweetened condensed milk

1 tablespoon (15 ml) almond extract

2 cups (250 g) raspberries, or (340 g) halved or quartered strawberries

1 cup (190 g) fresh lychees or canned lychees, drained, halved if larger than the berries

1   Oil a 9-inch (23 cm) square baking dish with almond oil or another nut oil, if you have it.

2   Sprinkle the gelatin over the warm water in a small saucepan. Turn the heat to low and stir continuously until the gelatin dissolves. Stir in the sugar until dissolved. Remove the pan from the heat and stir in the sweetened condensed milk and almond extract. Pour into the prepared dish and cool for 15 to 30 minutes. Refrigerate for at least 2 hours or until set.

3   Shortly before serving, cut the jelly into 1-inch (2.5 cm) squares. Divide the jelly squares among six martini glasses. Scatter portions of berries and lychees over all and serve soon.

THANKS

I have the best family. Heather Jamison Neale, JB Neale, and grandkids Riley, Bronwyn, and Chloe, you inspire me every day. Sisters Myrna Richard and Julie Alters Snodgrass, brothers-in-law John Richard, Joe Snodgrass, and Bob Jamison, and Bob's wife, Rose, are always there to help me in any way. And now there are a load of nephews, nieces, and even littler barbecue cooks and eaters coming up through the ranks.

The good folks at Foodways Texas, most importantly past board president Kelly Yandell, kept me up on all kinds of barbecue info, past and present. So many Texas pitmasters, chefs, and restaurateurs have fielded my pesky questions over time. I'm not listing them here because their numerous names are scattered throughout the text. I must make mention, though, Aaron Franklin, whose Austin barbecue I first stood in line for a decade ago, thoroughly convinced that his food couldn't be up to the then-modest amount of attention he was receiving. I felt struck by a lightning bolt as I dug into his brisket and other dishes. It was stupendous that day and every time since, truly setting the bar for consistency and quality. Aaron started a revolution and nearly single-handedly saved a great American cooking tradition from obscurity.

The other restaurant wizards I must mention are Lisa and Tom Perini, proprietors of Perini Ranch Steakhouse and friends through good times and sad. If you've not made a pilgrimage to their restaurant in Buffalo Gap, step away from your barbecue pit for one weekend and go. Or, order one of their mesquite-smoked peppered beef tenderloins and save yourself a lot of hot, smoky cooking (periniranch.com). The Perinis first introduced me to the faculty of Texas A&M University's Rosenthal Meat Science and Technology Center, most importantly Dr. Jeff Savell and Dr. Davey Griffin. There's not a shred of information about meat that these folks don't know. This team partners with Foodways Texas on Camp Brisket and Barbecue Summer Camp, two of the finest events a barbecue novice or pro could hope to experience. Camp Brisket ranks as one of my top food memories in a lifetime of unforgettable culinary opportunities.

My work has been made immeasurably easier and better informed because of a number of writers. Patricia Sharpe, culinary editor at *Texas Monthly*, was initially a mentor who later became a friend and, in both roles, has always encouraged me. *Texas Monthly* made an effing brilliant decision a few years back when it established a staff position for barbecue editor and hired Dallas architect Daniel Vaughn to fill it. I mention that he's an architect by training because he's given more structure to this subject than anyone else in the state. Daniel's extensive and passionate writing in the magazine, as well as in his book *The Prophets of Smoked Meat*, are essential to understanding and appreciating this art and craft we call Q.

Robb Walsh and I have been covering the barbecue beat for about the same amount of time. He has covered it better historically, especially in his book *Legends of Texas Barbecue Cookbook*. Jess Pryles's website and book *Hardcore Carnivore*, in addition to having one of the snappiest names ever, are a wealth of meat advice.

Lolis Eric Elie was researching his seminal book *Smokestack Lightning* at the time that my husband Bill and I were working on *Smoke & Spice*, and our paths crossed over barbecue. He and photographer Frank Stewart first helped me understand the scale of the contributions African-Americans have made to our country's barbecue heritage. More recently, the writing and research of Adrian Miller have helped me sharpen my focus on these often-unsung heroes. Wyatt McSpadden is technically a photographer, but he tells the story of Texas barbecue better than many writers, both in his own books and in those of other authors.

I want to give a shoutout to friends Carol Haugh Brejot and Roy Fuller, who have driven me all over Houston and yonder to enjoy the city and surrounding area's growing barbecue scene. My friend and colleague Alison Cook, restaurant critic for the *Houston Chronicle*, was invaluable for her spot-on assessments of dining establishments there. You might remember Wayne Whitworth, one of the founders of Houston's Pitts & Spitts, from the book's early chapters. He initially taught me to cook on an offset-firebox barbecue pit. I had no idea at the time that it would turn out to be one of my most valuable life skills.

Not everyone important to this project is in Texas. Thank you to my agent Doe Coover for always having my back. For someone who lives in Boston, Doe sure knows a lot about Q. I've finally learned to stop making bets with her that include brisket. Meathead Goldwyn, the Chicago-based barbecue genius behind the book *Meathead* and website amazingribs.com, actually came out to New Mexico and, though he may not know it, helped me decide to pen this book. My editor, Dan Rosenberg, is also Chicago based, and he put the idea into my head initially and helped shape it in invaluable ways. Thanks to the many other members of the Quarto team who had a role in getting this into print and out the door.

On the home front, I had support, help with shopping or recipes, and laughs from Don Banas, Cathy and Dan Barber, Randy Bell, Ken Bowling, Craig Carpenter, Juan Castillo, Lynn Cline and Kyle Langan, Susan Curtis, Cynthia Delgado and John Crant, Brad Furry and Bradyn Podhajsky, Jim Glover and Marianne Tenenbaum, Susie and Gayther Gonzales, Peter Imrick and Eric Bowyer, Raymond Knorpp, Kathryn Marshall, Linda Nelson and Randy McClanahan, Kyle Pacheco, Barbara and Bill Richardson, Jane Steele and Michael Heitz, Rachel Preston Prinz and Michael Prinz, Barbara and Bill Templeman, Angelina Vera and Raphael Shapiro, Jodi Vevoda and Will

Prull, Jayne Weiske, and probably another fifteen friends I am sure to be forgetting. Thank you for helping keep me fired up.

The barbecue recipes were tested on a variety of equipment. A Texas-size salute goes to Houston-based Pitts & Spitts, in particular, for their premier offset-firebox pit. Other equipment used included a Traeger pellet smoker, Hasty-Bake oven, Big Green Egg ceramic kamado, Cookshack electric smoker, Weber charcoal kettle, Ducane gas grill, and when appropriate, a Cameron Stovetop Smoker.

No list of acknowledgments would be complete without thanks to my late husband, Barbecue Bill Jamison, for his love of Texas food, history, and culture, vision for us as culinary writers, and unwavering support of me carrying it forward. The fire still burns. Love forever.

ABOUT THE AUTHOR

Cheryl Alters Jamison, four-time James Beard Award-winning author, had the misfortune to be born in Illinois where barbecue choices were limited. But as soon as she got the chance, she ran to Texas to live and indulge in amazing barbecued dishes. She grew a love for barbecued brisket the most . . . well except for when she is presented with beef short ribs, or pork ribs, or sausage links, or wings, or shrimp, or snapper, or . . . oh, never mind. You get the idea. Cheryl was eventually spirited away to the mountains of New Mexico where she married her late husband and coauthor Bill Jamison, a Texas Hill Country native. She now has relatives spread around Austin, San Antonio, Lubbock, and San Marcos. Cheryl is the author of over twenty cookbooks which include the landmark *Smoke & Spice*, *Texas Home Cooking*, *The Border Cookbook*, and *Texas Slow Cooker*. Cheryl recently wrote *Perini Ranch Steakhouse* cookbook with Buffalo Gap's Tom and Lisa Perini.

INDEX